D0274699

ARCHIE
A Biography of A. C. MacLaren

ARCHIE

A Biography of A. C. MacLaren

MICHAEL DOWN

London
GEORGE ALLEN & UNWIN
Boston   Sydney

44169997

First published in 1981

GEORGE ALLEN & UNWIN LTD
40 Museum Street, London WC1A 1LU

© Michael G. Down, 1981

British Library Cataloguing in Publication Data

Down, Michael
  Archie.
  1. Maclaren, A. C.
  2. Cricket players—England—Biography
  I. Title
  796.35'8'0924   GV915.M2/   80-42125

ISBN 0-04-796056-6

03946985

Set in 11 on 13 point Garamond by
Red Lion Setters, London, WC1N 2LA
and printed in Great Britain
by Billing and Sons Ltd., Guildford,
London and Worcester.

A. C. MacLaren lighted a fire in me never to be put out

Sir Neville Cardus

Contents

Illustrations

Acknowledgements
All the above illustrations were provided by Howard and Helen Kerridge,
except photographs 6-13 (the George Beldam Collection) and 17-18
(MCC) and the drawing on page 159 (Daily Mail).

Preface

'Why has there never been a biography of A. C. MacLaren?' This was the question which first prompted my interest in this fascinating character. For two years the task of attempting to correct the historical oversight has at times bordered on obsession, with endless hours spent scouring libraries and old newspaper files. So much about MacLaren had been forgotten, lost or distorted over the years that the writing of his biography became a search—at times frustrating, but at others immensely rewarding. One such highlight was undoubtedly the discovery of Archie's own, carefully preserved scrapbooks. Discussions with a few surviving acquaintances and relatives further helped to put flesh onto the bare bones of his cricketing deeds.

Throughout the research, numerous requests for assistance and information were sent to cricket enthusiasts and ex-players throughout the world. Almost without exception, the replies provided at least a clue, and often invaluable details or reminiscences. Briefly, I must acknowledge the major contributions of: Bob Arrowsmith, Gilbert Ashton, Sir Hubert Ashton, Robert Brooke, Geoffrey Copinger, David Frith, David Gallagher, H. S. T. L. Hendry, Howard and Helen Kerridge, W. O. G. Lofts, the late Malcolm Taylor, Gordon Tratalos and Bob Warburton. Space will not permit the listing of all the others who kindly rendered assistance. In addition, much information was culled from the staff and resources of the libraries at Old Trafford, Lord's, Mitcham and Manchester, and the BBC Written Archive Centre.

I am particularly indebted to Col Alex Wilkinson and Len Hopwood for their substantial contributions to the text, and to Philip Thorn for his invaluable assistance in making the book possible. The typescript was painstakingly prepared by my mother and by Denise Horvath.

Archie

Following the completion of the manuscript for *Archie*, two frustrating years passed before publication became possible. During that time the efforts of Philip Thorn, Peter Wynne-Thomas, David Frith and John McKenzie were much appreciated. Finally, however, it was John Newth of George Allen & Unwin (through the good offices of Charles Steggell) who provided Archie MacLaren with his rightful place in cricket literature.

Last, but far from least, my wife Margaret supplied constant advice, patience and encouragement, and like myself became rather fond of old Archie Mac.

MICHAEL DOWN

1
The Noblest Roman

The name of A. C. MacLaren has shone brightly through cricket's history for more than three quarters of a century. The vivid memory of his batsmanship and bearing frequently stirred cricket's peerless essayist, Sir Neville Cardus, to the pinnacle of his descriptive art. 'He was the noblest Roman of them all,' writes Cardus, and surely no cricketer ever earned a finer epitaph.

For more than thirty years MacLaren dominated every cricket field he set foot on, from his native Manchester to his favourite Sydney; he batted both majestically and successfully; for over a quarter of a century his world record individual score of 424 remained unsurpassed; he was captain of England against Australia more times than any other man before or since – and all this during one of cricket history's richest periods, the so-called Golden Age. Although he was a contemporary of Jessop, Ranji, Fry, Rhodes and Hirst, MacLaren's name never suffered by comparison with such heroes.

Yet despite his ability and success, his popularity with the public and the unconditional tributes by Cardus, the MacLaren story remains a strangely contradictory one. As one reads about him, the suspicion grows of certain unmentioned flaws in both his career and his character. There are repeated hints that although his majestic, almost arrogant countenance captivated many, relationships with others in the cricket world were less than harmonious. John Arlott summarised this impression: 'It was MacLaren's tragedy that all his virtues bred their own faults. He was strong but inflexible, intelligent but intolerant: single-minded but humourless: impressive on the field but often disappointingly petty off it.'

This contradictory nature explains why opinions of MacLaren are as varied as the people who express them. Many found him a marvellously attractive character whereas others place too much emphasis on the controversial incidents and disagreements that accompanied his career. Perhaps this dichotomy is understandable since, of the really prominent cricketers, he has been surely the most neglected biographically. This long overdue study of the man and his cricket will attempt to give a balanced view, somewhere between Cardus' 'incapable of a paltry gesture' and Arlott's 'disappointingly petty'.

Possibly it will in the end prove impossible to assess a man thirty-five years after his death when even during his own lifetime no two people reacted alike to him. Nevertheless, when the contemporary reports and the evidence of those few survivors who actually knew him are collected and sifted, a picture emerges of a rather likeable kind of rogue. As E. W. Swanton recalls, 'He was really an attractive rascal.'

Archie MacLaren first announced his cricketing brilliance in the summer of 1895, a noteworthy year in the history of the game. This season, which effectively marked the dawning of the Golden Age, was dominated by MacLaren and W. G. Grace – another 'attractive rascal' who at the age of forty-six enjoyed a glorious Indian summer, performing the unprecedented feat of scoring 1000 runs in May followed by his hundredth first-class century. While W.G. monopolised the headlines, the Lancashire County Cricket Club and its supporters were a trifle confused to find that the 23-year-old MacLaren, recently appointed county captain, had been forced by financial considerations to take a job at a preparatory school for the duration of the summer term. While Grace was reeling off century after century in the glorious weather of that distant summer, the young ex-Harrovian had to be content with practice against the bowling of his pupils.

When the school term finished, however, MacLaren journeyed

down from London to Taunton for his re-appearance in the Lanca-shire team against Somerset. It is history now how he stunned the cricketing world by amassing 424 to eclipse every record in the book and even steal the limelight from Grace himself. The details of this colossal innings are catalogued in Chapter 3 but here let us just recall one of the many congratulatory telegrams that poured into the small West Country pavilion. It read: 'Heartiest congratula-tions. Wish I had seen it. Must have been ripping. Was rather anxious about my record though – Stoddart.' These words by A. E. Stoddart, England's victorious and much-fêted captain of the previous winter's tour to Australia, capture so much that made the Golden Age the most evocative and fondly remembered period in cricket history. During that recent campaign in Australia, Stoddart and MacLaren had played cricket as tough and as unrelenting as any experienced by the modern professionals, yet they were amateurs. The significance of this is not simply that they were supposed to be unpaid (MacLaren certainly received money for playing) but that they were amateur in spirit. This same Stoddart had once scored 485 for Hampstead in a club game and he knew the mental and physical strain such a feat involved. Yet what was his considered comment? 'It must have been ripping.' This was the attitude that fostered Jessop, Trumper, MacLaren and all the rest.

This season of 1895 provided the springboard for Archie's long and distinguished career. In the space of twelve months he made a century in a Test match, scored his 424, completed three succes-sive centuries and even met his future wife. During the next ten years he was a dominant figure in the world of cricket, being undis-puted captain of England and one of the most attractive and successful batsmen in the history of the game. Of his English contemporaries only Ranjitsinhji and Jackson surpassed his record with the bat, while nobody led his country so many times. As Cardus' 'noblest Roman' he typified the Golden Age, although as captain and thinker he was years ahead of his time.

This contradictory character batted like an aristocrat, his manner and bearing on and off the field were aristocratic, yet he had not been born into the genuine upper classes. His family were by no means poor but their income sprang from a Manchester warehouse and shipping business – they were certainly not the idle rich. Yet by some quirk of his upbringing and heredity Archie believed that membership of that privileged class was his by right. Throughout his life he was as often as not virtually penniless yet he never allowed his attitude of grandeur to slip. As Cardus wondered, 'Where he got his flavours of blue blood from I never could tell or find out.' This background helps to explain Archie's somewhat curious nature.

In his dealing with people, cricketing and otherwise, could it be that he was over-correcting for a feeling of inferiority? 'He was never arrogant but at times unbearable,' said one friend. He could be a warm, amusing companion and a delightful raconteur, but on occasion he was awkward, high-handed and thoroughly unpleasant. In the cricket world this led him into endless controversies and rows. He was a tactless man and would say what he wanted with little regard for the consequences. Such was his way with everything, especially money. He was most unreliable and gained a reputation for borrowing from anyone, including the professionals who played under his captaincy. William Howard, a long-serving pavilion attendant at Old Trafford, told how one day everyone he met had the message that Mr MacLaren was looking for him and appeared to be in a bad mood. Everywhere he went it was the same story until eventually he discovered MacLaren sitting in the ladies' pavilion with his wife. On enquiring why Archie had wanted him he was told in a matter-of-fact way, 'I only wanted to borrow five shillings to buy my wife some chocolates but I found some money in your locker so I took that.' On another occasion MacLaren was threatened with expulsion from the MCC if he did not pay his subscription which had lapsed for some years.

In spite of these faults he was a charming man and remarkably generous on the infrequent occasions when he came into some money. At these times it would be champagne all round. Despite his strange habit of sometimes being extremely rude to people for no apparent reason, his many friends worshipped him whatever he did.

His shortage of regular income led him throughout his life to a succession of schemes and business ventures by which he hoped to make money. At various times he obtained income from, among other ideas: journalism; radio broadcasting; advertising; hotel ownership; bloodstock agent; banking; cotton merchant; marketing of cricket equipment, including the invention of pneumatic pads and bats made from imported Spanish willow; whisky salesman; motor-car salesman; film extra in Hollywood; cricket magazine editor; cricket coach; lecturing; hiring out cricket films; manager of a private team; schoolmaster; personal secretary to Prince Ranjitsinhji; assistant secretary to Lancashire CCC.

It can honestly be said that not one of these ventures was ever remotely successful, but Archie never tired of trying to interest people in his latest idea. William Howard recalled that 'to listen to Mr MacLaren's numerous schemes and ideas which he described in rather an egotistical manner was fascinating to some extent; but on my attempting to pass judgement upon them, he would often say, ''Damn you William! You are always trying to throw cold water on my ideas.'' '

Some of Archie's schemes do give an insight into his main interests in life. Chiefly, of course, he was fanatical about cricket; the tactics and strategy of captaining England were constantly on his mind and during the summer he would send out and receive reports from all over the country. Almost equally overwhelming was MacLaren's passion for horse racing. He was a meticulous student of handicapping and even owned horses at one time. He gambled regularly but this was not really the reason for his financial troubles since he rarely had much money to lose. Len Hopwood and the late Malcolm Taylor, two players who were under MacLaren's charge when he coached the Lancashire second XI in 1922, well remember his pre-occupation with the sport of kings. In conversation with the author, Hopwood vividly recollected the team's train journeys to away matches during which Archie would sit by himself studying a huge pile of racing papers. In a letter to the author, Taylor's reminiscence of Archie's racing exploits goes as follows: 'Mr MacLaren had his salary cheque

5

posted to him in Newcastle where we were playing Northumberland. On opening the letter it was for £200, much less than he had expected. His rage was so great that the Northumberland captain came up to see what was the matter. Old A.C. was livid. Then Mr Stanger-Leathes, who had a horse running that day at Jesmond, just said, ''Put the money on my horse, Archie.'' This he did and duly won £1000, but after three days he had lost the lot.'

Archie's other great interests were hunting and coursing, and over the years he owned many greyhounds. As far as riding was concerned, Ranji commented, 'He is fond of horses and imagines he can ride.' Ranji was a great friend of MacLaren's for many years and their sporting activities together even included tiger shoots in India.

Throughout his life Archie also maintained a great love of cars and motoring. In fact he enjoyed all the typical manly pursuits – sport, hunting, gambling, fast cars, alcohol (again not to the extent that it was a problem). He was also very attractive towards women and his natural charm made him pleasant company. At one time Nellie Melba was one of his closest friends, but despite being a ladies' man, he was devoted to his wife, Maud, and they remained happily married for almost fifty years. Maud, although small in stature, was very strong-willed and she certainly kept old Archie under control. MacLaren often used to go to auction sales and more often than not would come back with something that had caught his eye but was totally useless. On one such occasion Archie gathered together the whole family, took them down to the basement and unveiled his latest bargain – a full-size, Greek-goddess style statue which he was convinced was worth a fortune. Maud took one look before declaring that the thing was an eyesore which would not be allowed anywhere near the house. A dejected Archie was forced to hide the statue in the depths of their large garden in Berkshire, where it stands to this day.

Once during a match in New Zealand when two of the local batsmen looked like making a stand, Mrs MacLaren sent out a note to her husband suggesting a change in bowling. Archie was most indignant, declaring, 'For twenty-five years my wife has bossed me

in the house, but I'll be damned if she will do it on the cricket field.'
Needless to say, the change was made and proved successful.

One of Archie's great talents was talking. He was a marvellous
raconteur and could discourse on bygone Test matches almost
indefinitely (see cartoon on page 159). In his later years, even when
he was far from well, he loved to gather his old friends around him
and together they would become engrossed in their reminiscences.
Often these meetings ran long into the night and like so many
cricket enthusiasts, Archie would eventually have to be summoned
to bed by his long-suffering wife who would bang repeatedly on the
ceiling with her walking stick. During the war, when Sir Winston
Churchill was inspiring the nation, Archie loved to recall that
Churchill had been his fag at Harrow. When asked what he was
like, MacLaren would reply in his best upper-class accent, 'Snotty
little so-and-so.'

One of the MacLaren contradictions was that at various times he
would appear an eternal optimist and at others the most gloomy
pessimist. In fact he was basically an optimist at heart, especially
regarding his business ventures, but the idea spread that he was a
pessimistic captain who considered himself beaten before he had
begun. Certainly he would often complain about the selection of
the England team, but anyone who knew him realised that this was
simply his way and was intended semi-humorously. Ranjitsinhji
summed up much of MacLaren's character when he said, 'Archie
is a most amusing and agreeable companion. He affords much
amusement to us all by his queer sayings and witty remarks. He is
always cheerful and full of ''go''. He imagines he is unlucky in
everything, but Archie without his grumbling, as someone
remarked the other day, would be like curry without chutney.' The
effect this had on other people was once described by an acquaintance as follows: 'When a man makes a mannerism of grumbling,
with the assistance of a very dry humour, it is on the cards that he
will be popular with his intimates and the reverse with the rest of
his acquaintances.'

To sum up, MacLaren was at various times genial, charming and
humorous whilst at others he could be arrogant, high-handed and

7

imperious. His lofty self-assurance is best displayed by two oft-repeated cricketing stories. First, in a Roses game, George Hirst was running through the early Lancashire batting and making the ball swerve alarmingly. MacLaren alone was standing firm, and at the end of an over he approached Hirst and arrogantly remarked, 'You're bowling well, George, but not well enough.'

On another occasion Ted Wainwright, quoted by Cardus, reported an incident in a Gentlemen v. Players match: 'Mr MacLaren was on 49, and, as the match wasn't Lancashire v. Yorkshire, I bowled him an easy one to leg, but he kicked it away for one leg bye and came to my end and said, ''What's the meaning of sending me that rubbish?'' And I said, ''I was giving you one for your fifty, sir,'' and he said, proud like, ''I can hit the *best* you can bowl, Wainwright, or anybody.'''

Archie, then, was noble and impressive, but he inevitably rubbed certain people the wrong way and this brought down upon himself endless criticism – some of it unfair. To trace his cricket career and private life is to see just what a complex person he was; perhaps most of all, however, it is to recognise that MacLaren was one of the most attractive batsmen and possibly the greatest captain of all time.

2
Early Development

Archibald Campbell MacLaren was born, the second of seven brothers, on 1 December 1871 in Whalley Range, a fashionable suburb of Manchester. Archie was less than two years younger than his brother, James, and the pair were constant companions as children. Both were intensely keen on cricket, as were all the family.

Despite his name, Archie's ancestry was a mixture of Scottish, Irish and English, his father, James MacLaren senior, being a successful Manchester-based cotton merchant and shipping agent. As his children grew up, however, James allowed himself the luxury of spending less time at the business which he had inherited from his father, and more with his family. Eventually in 1889, at the age of only forty-four, he was able to hand over to his nephews and retire to Guernsey, where he devoted his spare time almost solely to rugby and cricket. He had begun to play rugby about the same time as he was married, aged nineteen, and with a number of other enthusiasts soon established the Manchester club, which rose to a prominent position. As well as playing, he also became one of the first northern members elected to the Rugby Union committee, and in 1882 held the office of President.

During the summer months Archie's father was equally busy, serving as honorary treasurer to the Lancashire County Cricket Club from 1881 until his death in 1900. He had played club cricket as a young man and was a good judge of a cricketer but it was as an administrator that he was most valuable. With Sam Swire, the secretary, he was largely responsible for running affairs at Old Trafford during this period. James MacLaren's business experience was invaluable in the post of treasurer, and his term of office brought unprecedented financial security. It was around this time that the negotiations for purchasing the Old Trafford ground were completed, although not without a serious disagreement between the secretary and treasurer. The well-liked Sam Swire considered the asking price too high but an alliance between A. N. Hornby and MacLaren carried the committee, and the deal which was to prove so successful was carried through. During negotiations the pavilion offices had been the scene of considerable animosity between the two men, both steadfastly refusing to work in the building when the other was present. Indeed, MacLaren senior had something of a reputation for being quick-tempered and excitable, a trait that in some measure was passed on to his famous son. His dislike of being interrupted at work was never more apparent than when he grabbed the club scorer, Lunt, and pushed him down a flight of stairs. Apparently, though, he was a quixotic character and could be immensely kind and generous. He would be sorry and upset for days after he had vented his temper on some innocent colleague.

Naturally enough, James MacLaren was determined that his sons would be given every possible opportunity to fulfil the sporting ambitions which he had for them. To this end the boys were entered for Harrow School but unfortunately, after James, Archie and Geoffrey, the expense became too great and the younger brothers had to settle for a more humble education.

From their very youngest days Archie and James were taken by their father, and more often by their mother, Emily, to Old Trafford to watch the county matches. In later years, Archie would often recollect being introduced to the players, especially W. G. Grace (a great friend of MacLaren senior), and was apparently so enthralled that his sole ambition was to emulate them. Even at the age of seven he would reply to the question, 'What do you want to be when you grow up?' with the answer 'A cricketer!' To this end the boys were given tremendous encouragement by all the members of the family; even their aunts were only too pleased to bowl at them in the garden (shades of W.G.). Incidentally, the large family house in Upper Chorlton Road still stands, although it has sadly deteriorated into a honeycomb of small flats and the garden where Archie first played cricket is now rambling and overgrown. The residents of today would find it hard to believe that in MacLaren's childhood Upper Chorlton Road was a private thoroughfare with a toll gate and was situated in open countryside. Unlike today's rather untidy suburb, Whalley Range was then a comfortable distance from the built-up area of Manchester.

The first serious move to develop the cricketing prowess learnt in the garden came when, at the ages of eleven and nine respectively, James and Archie were sent to Elstree school, which had a good reputation for cricket and was a well-known training ground for future Harrovians. Mr MacLaren senior, on the advice of A. N. Hornby, had meticulously mapped out his sons' future with the immediate goal being a place in the Harrow and Lancashire XIs. Predictably, both soon won places in the Elstree first team, and Archie notched up his first ever century, 109 against the Elstree village team.

It was whilst at prep school that Archie and James had their first formal cricket coaching. Indeed, the school was surprisingly well served with cricketing masters including C. P. Wilson, W. N. Roe, P. H. Morton, H. G. and E. F. S. Tylecote and G. R. Burge as well as the Rev. V. P. F. A. Royle who had known MacLaren's father at Old Trafford, Perhaps this list is not so surprising considering the care with which the school was chosen. In addition to this instruction at Elstree, MacLaren senior would arrange, indeed insist, that during the Easter holidays both boys spend a complete fortnight at the Old Trafford nets, where they were coached by the professionals. Each year he paid two of the best players to bowl at the boys. Thus they had the great advantage of being taught from the age of eleven by Lancashire players such as Pilling, Briggs and Mold, as well as the talented staff at Elstree.

Archie was captain of the Elstree team during his final year, and then in 1886 he went to join his elder brother at Harrow. Unhappily, in that first season he found it strange to be playing against boys several years his senior and he scarcely scored a run. In fact, amongst the Harrow cricketing fraternity his arrival had been keenly awaited and his conspicuous lack of success caused some harsh comment. His schoolmates called him a fraud, and Archie reached the depths of despair. The following year, though, he fortuitously found himself included as a last minute replacement in an early season trial game, and performed so well that he was included in the school first XI. Within weeks an innings of 100 against the Earl of Bessborough's XI secured his place in the great match of the season against Eton at Lord's. The first of his father's ambitions had been fulfilled.

The great crowd at Lord's can hardly have been very impressed by their very first view of young Archie, aged only 15½, standing 5ft 7ins and using a size 5 bat. They were soon to change their minds. He joined an inexperienced Harrow team containing only three of the previous year's XI, including F. S. Jackson and Archie's elder brother, James. Against this Eton could boast a proven combination spearheaded by H. R. Bromley-Davenport, claimed by Jackson to be the best boy bowler ever seen at Lord's. Archie was far from overawed, however, and although Harrow were completely outclassed and beaten by six wickets, he opened the batting and top-scored in both innings with 55 and 67. The cricket press took notice of him for the first time, commenting that 'he played with great judgement and confidence...Cricketers generally will look to his future with great interest.' Finishing the season at the top of the school averages, he must have looked forward to his remaining years at Harrow with every confidence. *Lillywhite's Annual*, however, expressed its concern regarding a rather weak stroke to leg; this was later to become his 'celebrated pull shot'.

The wet summers of 1888 and 1889 which followed must have been disappointing and puzzling for both Archie and his father. The terrible weather produced a succession of slow wickets, totally different from those on which he had been brought up at Elstree, and Archie was clearly ill at ease on them. He scarcely played a single worthwhile innings in either season, his successive scores at Lord's being 0, 14, 17 and 16, and each time he fell to the same bowler, H. W. Studd. Nevertheless the Lancashire authorities were keeping an eye on him, giving him a couple of trials with the Colts and the occasional club game for Manchester.

It was during these formative years that Archie was developing the singular batting technique that was to become so famous later on. Before his experience in these two wet summers Archie had been able to play forward with impunity to almost all deliveries that were not short enough to pull. On slower, wet wickets, though, his failure to master back play resulted in his being repeatedly caught out from mistimed drives. Late in 1889 he was advised to try prac-tising in the nets with the bat held only in his right hand. The effect of this was to make a front foot stroke virtually impossible and for Archie it was this simple ploy that really did the trick. After much diligent practice under the watchful eyes of the Earl of Bessborough and I. D. Walker, the first fruits became dramatically apparent in 1890, his final year at Harrow.

Appointed captain, Archie went from strength to strength. During the summer term he totalled over 500 runs for an average of 42.54, including a breathtaking innings of 140 against I Zingari. For the Lord's match against Eton, Harrow were strong favourites with six of the previous year's XI, whereas the opposition were all newcomers. But there had been heavy rain for several weeks before, and on the first day of the match further heavy showers prevented any play at all. On the Saturday, MacLaren lost the toss and Eton struggled to 108 on a very tricky wicket. Although Harrow fared scarcely any better with 133, they would have been in far greater trouble but for their captain. Opening the innings, he scored 76 out of 120 in under two hours and put on a truly master-ful display of wet wicket play for one so young. Although the match was left drawn, Archie had shown, in an innings which he regarded as easily the finest of his schoolboy career, how well he had devel-oped his technique. The strong forcing back play, which was to become such a feature of his armoury, was now apparent for the first time. This was also the first of many examples of MacLaren playing a lone hand while the rest of his team succumbed on an uncertain pitch.

MacLaren's days at school ended on a triumphant note with scores of 101, 72 and 54 during a Harrow Wanderers tour. He had not only captained the XI but had held the Ebrington Cup for batting in 1887 and 1890 and for fielding in 1888, 1889 and 1890. During the winter he had, like his brother, been a prominent footballer, captaining Champion House in 1889 and representing the school in 1888 and 1889. In his last winter, however, he was unable to play because of a knee injury which was to trouble him again much later in his cricket career.

The rapid development of Archie's powers is mirrored in the seasonal Harrow batting averages.

Year	Inns	N.O.	Runs	H.S.	Ave.
1887	11	0	307	100	27.91
1888	14	0	132	28	9.43
1889	12	0	176	49	14.67
1890	13	0	553	140	42.54

Despite these achievements at school, the season of 1890 had really only just begun for 18-year-old Archibald MacLaren. On Thursday 14 August the Lancashire committee invited him to play for the county first team against Sussex at Brighton. This was not intended to be a daunting introduction to first-class company, since Sussex were firmly entrenched at the foot of the county table whereas the Red Rose county was fighting out the Championship battle in third place. Nevertheless, for a boy who had only been out of school for a matter of weeks to be pitched into the presence of Hornby, Barlow, Briggs and Mold must have been quite unnerving. Even as a boy, though, Archie possessed the same belief in his own ability that was to become his chief hallmark in later years, and he showed no sign of apprehension.

Sussex, batting first on an unreliable surface, were predictably shot out for 86 by Arthur Mold (six for 59). In reply Lancashire were faring no better, having lost Barlow and F. H. Sugg for 9, when the new recruit strode confidently to the wicket. As in the recent Harrow v. Eton game, Archie proceeded to take the bowling by the scruff of the neck, despite the rapid fall of wickets at the other end, and in just two and a quarter hours he saved the side with a brilliant 108 out of 189. The innings was not only chanceless, but contemporary accounts credit the youngster with scarcely even a mishit. It was straight out of the pages of the *Boy's Own Paper*. Johnny Briggs weighed in with 54, Lancashire totalled 248 and Sussex were soon dismissed a second time by Mold and Watson for just 100. Although many other players have scored a century on debut in first-class cricket, perhaps we should note that time of two and a quarter hours. This was obviously no nervous boy feeling his way against grown men.

As is the way of things, the overjoyed Archie was brought down to earth with a bump in the very next match. Lancashire's championship hopes were ruined when they were caught on a wet Oval wicket, and succumbed by an innings and 76 runs to the all-conquering Surrey team of this period; Archie failed to reach double figures. This was followed by a duck against Kent at Beckenham and scores of 17 and 10 against Nottinghamshire in his first match at Old Trafford. Both of these games were on poor, rain-affected pitches and perhaps showed that there was still work to be done on MacLaren's free-driving technique when confronted with a slow wicket. Anyhow, thanks to that first century, he finished fourth in the Lancashire averages and everyone looked forward to great things.

A significant difference between Archie and almost all the other famous amateurs of his day was that on leaving school he did not go up to University. The reason was simply financial. We have seen that it was with some effort that MacLaren senior had been able to send three sons to Harrow, so to attempt to pay for any of his seven boys to go to Oxford or Cambridge was out of the question. Archie resigned himself, doubtless rather reluctantly, to a position in the Manchester and Liverpool District Bank. This also had an adverse effect on his cricketing development. Whilst Jackson, Fry, Jessop and the rest were gaining the varied experience of playing University cricket during the summer term and then joining their counties, MacLaren's appearances were strictly limited.

The temptation to play gradually became overwhelming, however – five games in 1891, thirteen in 1892, and eighteen in 1893. If it had not been for his 'couldn't care less' attitude towards money, he would surely have been lost to the game of cricket. Without the advantage of a private income he really should have buckled down to working for a living, but Archie always adopted the philosophy of 'something will turn up', and it usually did.

Despite his frequent absences, the years 1891–3 were ones of gradual improvement and of reasonable, though not outstanding, success. The restricted opportunities of his second county season did not stop him heading the Lancashire batting averages and in the following year, 1892, he registered another century – 135 against Gloucestershire at the Aigburth ground in Liverpool, later the stage of many of his finest innings. There were lean periods, though, and towards the end of this season the selection committee were in favour of resting him. Hearing of this via his father, Archie pleaded to be given another chance in the next game. This was against Sussex at Brighton, the scene of his initial success. Given the opportunity to open the innings, he concentrated as never before while scoring 132 in three and three-quarter hours. He gave only one chance, at 103, and at last it seemed that his form had returned. Ironically, his weak knee collapsed under the strain and he was forced to miss the last few games of the season just as his perseverance had been rewarded. This was the first of a long series of injuries and minor ailments which were to hamper his play continually in England, and especially so in his later years, when he often captained the side despite being too ill to bat or field properly.

These were erratic years in the fortunes of Lancashire. Although runners up in 1891 and 1893, they were very disappointing in 1892. Everything really depended on the bowling of Mold and Briggs, while the batsmen of the future such as Johnny Tyldesley, MacLaren and Albert Ward were only just beginning their careers. The old order, led by Hornby and Barlow of long ago, were fading out and the captaincy was not settled. Whenever young Archie did play under Hornby, however, he was invariably impressed and indeed influenced by the 'iron man' of Old Trafford. Although often known as 'Monkey' (due to weighing only six and a half stone when playing for Harrow), Hornby's other nickname of 'Boss' probably described him better. An effervescent, strict captain, he served the county for over thirty years as a player before holding the presidency of the club until 1916. In Archie's first game at Brighton, Hornby asked the new recruit where he fielded. MacLaren, possibly rather full of himself, replied, 'Oh, anywhere except point', and proceeded to find himself at point for the duration of the innings. This response was typical Hornby and there is just a little of MacLaren in it as well. Indeed, the hard and dominating characters of the two men were remarkably similar in many ways.

After spending the winter of 1892–3 in New Orleans trying to learn about the cotton business, Archie returned to a much fuller season and although failing to reach a three-figure score, he made important strides in the eyes of the Victorian cricketing public. In the Roses match he stood alone in scoring 54 out of a total of only 169 which was enough to win by an innings. Returning to Aigburth for the visit of Somerset, he captained the side for the first time in the absence of the amateurs Hornby, Crosfield and Kemble. The 21-year-old acquitted himself like a veteran, winning both the toss and the match.

One newspaper was moved to write: 'The young amateur is about the most consistent scorer in the eleven, and wherever he goes he wins golden opinions. Some critics may occasionally wish him to get runs faster, but none take exception to his style.' This last gentle rebuke seems strange in the light of MacLaren's subsequent reputation, but we should note that at this stage all the games which he missed were against the weaker counties. His availability being limited, he made sure that his appearances were put to the best possible use.

Perhaps most important of all, and certainly most important for his ever prouder father, were the representative honours that came

Archie's way. Selected to open the batting for the North of England against the touring Australians, MacLaren and his county colleague, Albert Ward, put on 121 in eighty minutes for the first wicket, of which Archie scored 66. These two young batsmen were contrasting in many ways, the professional Ward having first played for Yorkshire in 1886 before becoming a Lancashire regular in 1889. He reached cricketing maturity a little ahead of MacLaren and this year saw him selected for all three Test matches. In fact, Ward only appeared in the last two Tests, and it is not widely known that he turned down the opportunity of his debut in the Lord's match so that he could assist Lancashire. The club minutes contain an order to give Ward £4 as the difference in payment between the two games. Over the next ten years these two were to launch many a Lancashire innings together, Ward's solid, dependable style proving the ideal foil for MacLaren's more direct methods.

Shortly after this first success against the tourists, a telegram for Mr A. C. MacLaren arrived at Old Trafford. The telegram, which is still carefully preserved, read simply, 'Will you play Gentlemen versus Players here – Perkins.' The honour of taking part in this fixture at Lord's, second only to a full England cap, was the first vital step in MacLaren's international career. The game was drawn, with Archie batting at number six and struggling to 21 in an hour and twenty minutes. Perhaps more important, it gave him the taste of big match atmosphere and an opportunity of playing alongside A. E. Stoddart and under the captaincy of W. G. Grace.

The following season of 1894 was crucially important in the early development of MacLaren. Although his batting did not set the world alight, he at last gave up the unequal struggle between cricket and business, appearing in all Lancashire's matches. He also took over the captaincy when things were looking black for the county and made such a success of the job that he was already being thought of as a future England skipper. After he had appeared again for the Gentlemen in the prestige match at Lord's, the season was brought to a thrilling climax by his selection as a member of A. E. Stoddart's touring side to Australia.

Lancashire started the season in terrible form, losing six of their first seven championship fixtures. S. M. Crosfield had been elected captain for the year, but he was not always available. For the first nine matches he shared the duties with A. N. Hornby and A. T. Kemble until all three dropped out in turn, leaving the team completely disorganised. The players and spectators became increasingly despondent. MacLaren was the only amateur available who had any experience of county cricket, and towards the end of June he was appointed the new captain almost by default. He had been in terrible batting form, and his captaincy started disastrously at Trent Bridge. He lost the toss and after half an hour Arthur Mold, the county's main weapon, retired with a strained ankle. The match was eventually lost by an innings, to be followed by another defeat against Kent at Tonbridge. The critics were only too keen to judge the 22-year-old captain a failure but in the next game, against Derbyshire, the team rallied to win in a close finish. In this match the Lancashire batting was opened by the MacLaren brothers, but unfortunately J.A. with scores of 0 and 3 could never match Archie. Although he had captained Harrow in his last year, his four games for Lancashire between 1891 and 1894 yielded him little success. James MacLaren's talents lay elsewhere and in the year 1900 he qualified as a doctor.

The next game, against Somerset at Old Trafford, was won in a single day's play and by the end of the season the county were a match for anybody, finishing fourth in the table. Only one of the last twelve games under MacLaren was lost. Although Archie did not manage a century and was only sixth in the Lancashire averages, the *Manchester Guardian* noted that: 'Mr MacLaren has steadily maintained his reputation as a batsman, and has done some brilliant bits of fielding.' The *Manchester Courier* acknowledged the skilful way in which the youngster had led his team: 'Mr MacLaren has some reason to be proud of the work achieved since he assumed command towards the end of June.'

By far the closest game for the young skipper to handle had been the fixture with Surrey at the Oval which ended in a tie. Unfortunately, feelings ran high during the match and Archie was obviously still annoyed when he wrote in his scrapbook, 'Thanks to some disgraceful bustling of the umpires on the part of Surrey's wicket-keeper Wood, this match ended in a tie. Henty was the offending umpire. Blindness and deafness being the cause of his incapacity.' MacLaren's rather candid notes also contain details of four Lancashire batsmen who were given out caught when they had apparently not touched the ball, plus a claim that Street, who scored 48 out of Surrey's first innings of 97, was rightfully dismissed at 0 and 23.

This season of 1894 closed, then, despite its ups and downs and moments of anxiety, with MacLaren established as captain of Lancashire at the remarkably young age of twenty-two. His last-minute selection for Stoddart's team was the icing on the cake, and as the side set sail on the *Ophir*, so Archie was setting out on his long career as an international cricketer. This trip by Stoddart's men was to be the beginning of modern-style tours, with full press coverage and five Test matches: the beginning, in fact, of the Golden Age that was to follow.

Archie's acceptance of the invitation to tour under the normal terms of out-of-pocket expenses was helped considerably by the Lancashire committee's decision to advance him £100 out of club funds. This payment, noted in the club minutes, was the first of many to be made by the club, enabling Archie to continue playing regularly over the years.

The opportunity to visit Australia was fortunate for Archie in another very different way, since on the outward sea voyage he met and fell in love with his future wife, an Australian socialite named Maud Power. On arrival in Australia the couple found a leading society column referring to the 'Scotch-named member of the team who was her devoted companion throughout the voyage'.

Stoddart's side consisted of only thirteen players, of which two were wicket-keepers. Since W. A. Humphreys, the 45-year-old lob bowler, was not included in any of the Tests, this meant that Archie was certain of a place in all five matches, a luxury which no young player could hope for today. The strength of the side, and it *was* a strong one, lay in the bowling quartet of Richardson,

Lockwood, Peel and Briggs – all in their prime and arguably the finest combination ever to represent England's attack. The story of the Test matches has been dramatically told by Richard Binns in his entertaining book, *Cricket in Firelight*, and an overall tour description is included in the biography of A. E. Stoddart written by David Frith, so let us concentrate on MacLaren's part in this historic series.

Archie was odd man out in the first important match of the tour, against South Australia, which the Englishmen lost by six wickets despite totalling 476. From Adelaide the party travelled east and it was at the mighty Melbourne ground that MacLaren first walked out to an Australian wicket in a first-class game. Again the team was in trouble. After winning the toss, Stoddart had seen Ward, Brown and Brockwell shot out by the jubiiant Trott brothers and now it was up to the two amateurs to restore the balance. The natural reaction of both men was to launch a spirited counter-attack which proved so successful that 190 were added before the captain departed for 77. Bobby Peel joined Archie and the latter continued remorselessly to plunder the tired bowling. By the close of play the score was 379 for four, of which MacLaren had run up 220 not out, easily the highest and best innings of his brief career. He had also made history as the first batsman to score 200 in a day in Australia.

Skipper Stoddart cannot have had a quicker or more resounding confirmation of his judgement in selecting such an inexperienced young man. MacLaren played faultless cricket, not giving a chance until he reached 170, and in so doing became a firm favourite with the spectators and the press. On several occasions during the innings Archie had a drink brought out to him and much curiosity was aroused 'respecting the nature of the stimulant employed'. The youngster's popularity increased even more when it was revealed by a Melbourne newspaper that he had 'absorbed three Galley whisky and sodas during his innings'.

Next morning he soon fell for 228, and the local pundits were unanimous in proclaiming this the finest innings ever seen on the Melbourne ground. The crowd of 12,000 saw the England team turn out easy winners despite two missed catches in the deep by MacLaren. Archie had always been renowned for his athletic and safe fielding in the deep, so he was particularly embarrassed during the first few matches by his inability to judge the flight of high catches. This effect of the brilliant sunlight in Australia was one which he was most careful to practise against on his subsequent tours.

After taking part in good victories over New South Wales and Queensland (against whom he scored 74 not out), Archie was set to make his Test match debut on the Sydney Cricket Ground, later to become the scene of his greatest triumphs. This first match has since become legendary, not for MacLaren's initial appearance nor for that of his great Australian contemporary, Joe Darling, but for the recovery that enabled England to win the game despite following on 261 runs behind on the first innings.

On the first morning Tom Richardson at his most overpowering launched the series by clean bowling the first three Australians for 21, including Darling first ball. In fact, of Richardson's thirty-two victims in the forthcoming series, no less than twenty-six were to be clean bowled. Tall scores by Giffen and Syd Gregory led the comeback which finally totalled 586. It was mid-afternoon on the second day before the Lancashire pair, MacLaren and Ward, stepped out of the pavilion to set about England's reply in overcast conditions more reminiscent of their native Manchester. Archie had scored only 4 runs against the formidable attack of Ernest Jones and Charlie Turner – fiercer bowling than he had ever encountered before – when, with the score at 14, he went for his drive and only managed to spoon a terrible shot to Reedman at cover. Jones, the natural successor to Spofforth, was truly fast and F. S. Jackson regarded him as the finest quick bowler he had ever faced. In England in 1896 Jones so scared the renowned Nottinghamshire pair of Arthur Shrewsbury and William Gunn that it was said they both deliberately nudged catches to slip and were on their way to the pavilion before the fielder's hands made contact with the ball.

On the third day, despite several worthwhile contributions, England were asked to follow on but this time MacLaren and Ward saw off the new ball and took the score comfortably to 44 before Archie's inexperience and a lapse of concentration saw him beaten by the wily Giffen's slower ball. This was just the start Stoddart needed and by the fifth day he was able to set Australia 177 to win, thanks mainly to the dogged Albert Ward who added 117 to his first innings 75. At the close of that day, with the score 113 for two and Giffen and Darling well set, the game looked virtually over. Then, to the consternation of the Australians but the delight of Bobby Peel, it rained heavily all night and the dawn brought bright sunshine. These vital ingredients for a traditional Australian sticky wicket meant that the rest of the innings melted away on the sixth and final day for a total of just 166. Peel and Johnny Briggs were the heroes of one of the most amazing transformations in the history of cricket.

One interesting sidelight to the events of that dramatic last morning is that Peel and Lockwood, thinking the match already lost, had been socialising well into the night and at the appointed hour were nowhere to be seen. The Australian captain, Jack Blackham, chivalrously agreed to delay the start until they arrived at twenty minutes past twelve, thereby helping to seal his own fate. On this last day MacLaren again had trouble judging the high ball and dropped a catch late in the innings. Then, with two wickets to fall and only about a dozen runs needed for victory, Ernest Jones drove a skier to Archie on the rails at deep long-off. To his immense relief Archie this time clung on to the catch and the match was as good as over.

Before the second Test in Melbourne the team made the acquaintance of two promising youngsters named Trumper and Noble, who played for XVIII Sydney juniors and scored 67 and 152 not out respectively. The tourists also paid a Boxing Day visit to Randwick Races where Archie was very much to the fore. His passion for horse racing was well-known and it was no coincidence that the girl he had become so friendly with on board ship was the daughter of one of the leading racing officials in Australia.

The jubilation of the Test match victory and the pleasant social life was slightly marred for Archie at this point since he was already running out of spending money. The out-of-pocket expenses paid by the tour management, even with the £100 from the Lancashire club, did not meet Archie's needs. A good idea of where his money went can be gleaned from the fact that his own scrapbook of the tour contains far more cuttings concerned with the handicapping of racehorses than with cricket. Archie did not worry about his impecunious state, of course; he simply shrugged his shoulders and sent a telegram to whoever might help. One such was received by the Lancashire club who immediately dispatched a cheque to Australia.

The second Test was again won by England, thanks to surely the finest innings of A. E. Stoddart's career. His 173, after both sides had been dismissed cheaply in the first innings, put the game safely out of Australia's reach. MacLaren again failed to make his mark in either innings, in fact he lost his wicket to the very first ball of the game, delivered by Coningham in this curious character's only Test appearance. His opening delivery popped up from the wet surface and the batsman's tentative forward prod could only steer the ball into point's grateful hands. In the second innings MacLaren fared little better, scoring 15 before C. T. B. Turner uprooted his off stump. MacLaren later wrote, 'Turner had a fascination for me that no other bowler possessed. I could not take my eyes off him when he was bowling.' Certainly this short, thickset man with the strangely square-on bowling action was a distinct thorn in the young batsman's Test match progress.

Although Archie's form showed a distinct improvement at Adelaide, Australia won easily. On the first day the home team made 238, leaving MacLaren and Johnny Briggs ten minutes batting which they survived. The next day there was a substantial collapse but young Archie grimly held on, scoring 25 out of 56 before being fifth out, bowled by a delivery from Callaway which kept low. In the second innings Australian batsmen hammered an exhausted England attack to the tune of 411 but it was the unbearable heat which contributed most to the poor showing in the field. With England chasing an impossible target MacLaren chose to assert his authority over the bowlers for the first time in the series.

Opening with Albert Ward again, he stroked a majestic 35 out of the first 50 before being caught in the deep – the first of Albert Trott's eight victims. England were dismissed for a miserable 143 and Archie was one of the few batsmen to make any sort of show against the almost unplayable, rising off-breaks of the younger Trott, who was making his Test debut.

After a couple of country matches it was soon back to Sydney for the serious business of the vital fourth Test. Stoddart won the toss and after some thought asked Trott's men to bat first on a rain-affected wicket. The wisdom of the decision was plain with Australia slumping to 51 for six but a delayed start had given the wicket longer to dry and Graham, Darling (dropped by MacLaren but out next ball) and Albert Trott carried the total to 284. Writing years later, MacLaren still vividly recalled Harry Graham's match-winning innings: 'I can see Harry Graham darting forth from his crease to drive Tom Richardson . . . I think it was the finest century ever witnessed by me . . . Graham obtained more runs than we reckoned the whole eleven would make.'

With only ten minutes left to play out on the first day, MacLaren showed his inexperience and was inexcusably stumped off the elder Trott's teasing leg-break, but it was heavy overnight rain (which caused the abandonment of the second day's play), followed by all-important sunshine, that led to England's cheerless total of 65. None of the team could recall a wicket worse than the one on which Ward and J. T. Brown launched the follow on. Although dropped down the order, MacLaren was soon at the crease but immediately hooked Giffen straight into Bruce's hands to make the score 5 for three, last man 0. The remainder was a procession and Australia's innings victory had levelled the series without even the necessity to call on Albert Trott to bowl a single ball.

Between Tests, Archie scored a rapid 106 against a combined New South Wales and Queensland team, putting on a brilliant display of all-round hitting. His confidence for the final game was doubtless boosted not only by this innings but also by the receipt of another cheque from the Lancashire club. The committee also passed a resolution which provided both good and bad news for

Archie. The bad news was that the club saw fit to fix his expenses for the following season at £3 per week for twenty weeks; the good news was that this total of £60 would be sent to him in advance in Australia, enabling him to make the return journey in comfort.

So to Melbourne for the crowning glory of this finely balanced series of five classic games. The great fight-back by the Australians fully justified the innovation of the five-match series, which henceforth became the norm in Australia, with England following suit in 1902. The interest generated for this deciding match was unprecedented.

On a more personal note, Archie had failed to reproduce in the Tests the excellent form he had shown in the state and country games. With an average of only 12.50 in his eight innings for England, he would certainly have been dropped had there been a suitable replacement available; but there was no choice but to include him in the vital last match in Melbourne. As a compromise Stoddart changed his batting order to include Archie at number five with Billy Brockwell becoming the reliable Albert Ward's new opening partner. This adjustment was made to appear rather academic when Giffen won the toss and Australia put 414 on the board by mid-afternoon on the second day. In reply Brockwell fared no better as opener than Archie had and was soon stumped for 5. Stoddart then rallied his team but with just under an hour left the innings – and the series – were in the balance at 112 for three. MacLaren marched determinedly out to join Yorkshire's Johnny Brown with the 29,000 noisy spectators thirsting for more wickets before the close. Fortunately Archie settled in immediately and was soon playing the slow spin of Trott with such confidence that at stumps the score was a much healthier 200 for four, MacLaren 40 not out. His partner was now Bobby Peel who had scored (or not scored) four noughts in the last two Tests.

Next morning Archie soon reached his fifty in only sixty-five minutes, and then consciously set himself not to give his innings away. His scoring slowed while he dug himself in, a style totally foreign to him, but it showed that some lessons had been learned about international cricket during the last few frustrating months.

Peel gave him sterling support, scoring 73 while 162 were added in even time, and by lunch MacLaren had advanced to 78 having survived a caught and bowled chance to George Giffen at 69. Eventually at 2.50pm after nearly three hours of concentration, he drove Albert Trott for four to reach his first Test match century. During the next half-hour he lost Peel and survived chances to Jarvis behind the wicket and another hot return to Giffen before eventually treading on his wicket in the act of pulling a ball from Harry Trott. MacLaren had scored 120 in three hours and forty minutes of indefatigable resolution, and it was mainly due to his determined efforts that England finished a mere 29 behind on the first innings.

On the fourth day Australia could not force home this advantage in the face of heroic bowling by Tom Richardson and Bobby Peel. Nevertheless, the 297 eventually required for England to win the match and the series seemed a long way off. Despite Archie's first-innings success, Stoddart stuck to the same batting order and it is now history how J. T. Brown and Albert Ward put on 210 in 145 minutes to ensure an English victory. Brown's innings of 140 was nothing short of phenomenal and was far and away the pinnacle of his career. He set off at a great pace with a succession of vicious cuts and pulls and while Ward added just 5 Brown reached 50 in twenty-eight minutes. Several publications have since quoted thirty-eight minutes, but the shorter time appears from contemporary reports to be more accurate. The victory which he made possible was completed by MacLaren (20 not out) and Peel (15 not out), the total of 298 coming in only 215 minutes.

The tour had been a marvellous success for Stoddart's team, and for Archie. After a long struggle he had eventually triumphed, finishing the season fourth in the national batting averages behind Stoddart, Giffen and Hill. When the Orient liner *Orizaba* finally docked at Tilbury, MacLaren expressed his satisfaction with the tour in an interview which appeared in the *Manchester Guardian*. Commenting on his own play, he ascribed his success to the superior wickets which were common in Australia, adding that the double century against Victoria was his best innings. The hundred in the last decisive Test he casually dismissed as 'lucky', although he considered the hit wicket decision rather unfair since the bail was dislodged in the act of setting off for a run. Of the other players, Brown's innings was the greatest he had ever witnessed, and his Lancashire colleague Albert Ward 'batted like a book'. MacLaren also observed that it took Tom Richardson at least a month before he could adjust his length for the faster wickets and thereby achieve the amazing success that helped win the series.

Archie had learnt much about captaincy from A. N. Hornby, and now during the long Australian summer he took careful note of Stoddart's tactics. On this and the next tour MacLaren was deeply impressed by 'Stoddy' both as a cricketer and as a man: 'He stood out supremely great so often, and I experienced some of my greatest treats when his partner. His kindness to me was such that I always felt I could never do enough to make myself worthy of his affection.'

By contrast, MacLaren found much of Giffen's strategy puzzling and felt that despite the euphoria over England's victory, the Australians were a better overall team. One of the mistakes they made was to include McKibbin instead of Turner in the last Test, apparently because he had bowled Giffen in a state game at Sydney. Not only was Turner still a very great bowler but he had a distinct psychological edge over many of the English batsmen and MacLaren suggested that had he played, 'we might just have left those Ashes instead of bringing them back'. Regarding the other Australians, English readers were assured that for future reference, 'Callaway can't bowl a bit'.

From a wider standpoint the tour, especially the spectacular fifth Test, announced in ringing tones the dawning of the Golden Age to come, an age in which Archie was to be a central figure and which he was about to help launch with one of its most remarkable scoring feats.

3
424

Returning late from Australia via Japan, Archie missed the opening Lancashire fixture of 1895 but was available for the championship game with Leicestershire, scoring 23 and 6. This was followed by two uncharacteristic failures in the Roses match at Sheffield. At this time Archie was presented with the opportunity of taking a job as a schoolteacher at Mr Hastings' preparatory school in Harrow and was therefore forced to miss Lancashire's next eight games. Today, in our professional-oriented cricket world, this may seem an amazing thing for the county captain to do, but Archie was no doubt on the breadline after his winter in Australia; at least this type of employment would enable him to play in the school holidays. It also allowed him his first taste of coaching young cricketers, a passionate interest in his later years.

Nevertheless, this move by Lancashire's new captain and recently successful Test match batsman was far from popular with local supporters. If Archie ran true to form there is no doubt that the murmurings of disapproval fell on deaf ears. Although during his absence the strong county side kept up their bid for the championship and were never out of the first three, they lost three vital matches under the captaincy of S. M. Tindall and they certainly welcomed Archie back for the fixture with Somerset at Taunton on Monday 15 July.

Archie hurried down to the West Country at the close of the Eton and Harrow game at Lord's, and next day met up with his father who intended to watch his son's return to first-class cricket. Winning the toss, MacLaren took his fellow winter tourist, Albert Ward, with him to open the innings against a Somerset team playing their first season in the championship. Although an erratic side, they had met with some success under the captaincy of S. M. J. Woods, the Australian Test all-rounder, but in the previous game their bowling had been trounced to the tune of 692 by Essex.

It was just five minutes past twelve when the match started, 'in delightful weather, but in the presence of a small company', according to the *Manchester Evening News*. Archie, who had not batted against anybody over the age of fourteen for five weeks, came within a whisker of being bowled by the first ball of the match from the left-handed Tyler.

The new ball was shared by Woods who, with Tyler, was selected for the team which represented England in South Africa during the following winter. Of the two, Woods was the more expensive, MacLaren twice cutting him for four until at 39 Lionel Palairet, more famous for his cultured batting, replaced him. Ward reached his 50 out of 93 and was now dominating the bowling, allowing Archie to find his feet and play himself in comfortably. After reaching his own 50, though, MacLaren speedily caught and passed his partner's score. By lunch eight different bowlers had already been tried but the score stood on 141 for no wicket in just under two hours – MacLaren 72 and Ward 64.

Fortunately for Somerset the interval broke the batsmen's spell and in Tyler's first over after lunch Ward was caught at slip with the total unaltered. This brought A. G. Paul out to join his captain and any hopes of a breakthrough were firmly quenched as the pair immediately began to cut loose. In no time two cuts to the boundary brought up MacLaren's century and another saw the score pass 200 for one. Paul reached his fifty in an hour and the headline in the afternoon edition of the *Manchester Evening News* read, 'Extraordinary scoring'.

All the bowlers came alike to the pair, even Lionel Palairet's desperate resort to lobs only succeeding in bringing up the 300 at

4.25pm. Then came the most sensational period of the day as Tyler and Gamlin shared the bowling. Paul drove the former right out of the ground for six and not to be outdone, MacLaren repeated the treatment in Gamlin's very next over. First one player and then the other would be in the limelight and soon Paul's century and MacLaren's double were posted.

After a five-minute break for drinks, there being no tea interval in those days, Palairet's lob bowling finally did the trick by having Paul caught at deep long-on for a remarkable 177. The pair had put on 363 in three hours and ten minutes, only 35 short of Shrewsbury's and Gunn's world record partnership for any wicket, and the total was beyond 500. It says much for Paul, who had only recently scored his maiden century and was usually regarded as a defensive player, that he did not suffer by comparison with MacLaren. Just to show that Lancashire were still taking the game seriously a nightwatchman, Hallam, was sent in, but he soon fell to Palairet and at the close Archie had moved on to a massive 289 not out with the total towering at 555 for three in only five and a half hours.

By now the headline in the later editions of the *Manchester Evening News* had changed to 'Phenomenal scoring'.

That season of 1895 was W. G. Grace's great Indian Summer during which, at the age of forty-six, he completed a hundred centuries and became the first man to score a thousand runs in May. This achievement owed much to an innings of 288 against this same Somerset team, and with this score beaten and his world record 344 in danger the Great Man sent the following telegram to Taunton: 'Hearty congratulations on Archie's grand performance hope he will break record.' Amongst the other messages was one from Stoddart, 'Am speaking to everyone of my *friend* Archie. Well played, hope this will find you not out and going strong.' These and similar good wishes from others gave MacLaren all the incentive he needed on the second day of the game, which began at 11.35am in dull and overcast weather.

Starting where he had left off the previous evening, and unable to declare even if he had wished to (it was not until 1910 that a captain could declare at any time on the second day of a game), Archie's score soon passed 300 with an off drive for four off Tyler. At 12.45 the great moment arrived when W. G. Grace's enormous record was passed, and by lunch Archie was beyond the 400 mark and the total stood at 756 for four. He had scored over a hundred before lunch, and for the first time began to show signs of tiredness. Finally, with the total on 792, he was seventh out for 424, caught in the deep by Fowler off the bowling of the 17-year-old Gamlin, more famous as an England rugby union fullback. Gamlin's cricket career was limited to the two traumatic games of this week, against Essex and Lancashire, and one the following season against Yorkshire. His career bowling figures were two wickets for 207 runs and in six innings he managed four noughts followed by 2 and 5.

MacLaren's mammoth innings had included one six (out of the ground), 64 fours, 10 threes, 26 twos and 80 singles and in all he batted for seven hours fifty minutes – 470 minutes for 424 runs. The score sequence was as follows:

    11314114111411111111141112142431144142424112211 2
    414 – 101 (155 mins)
    24311441121414421144213221114414 1464414 – 200 (260
    mins)
    13442444111444141141144444431241111341 – 300 (350
    mins)
    4414141411213124224 – 346 (400 mins)
    42411142414244312211141 – 400 (444 mins)
    11112342144 – 424 (470 mins).

The four centuries came in 155, 105, 90 and 94 minutes.

This sequence, which differs considerably from that given in several contemporary and subsequent publications, is the one which was provided at the time by the Lancashire secretary, S. H. Swire, from the official club scorebook.

The poor Somerset bowlers would have been spared considerable extra punishment had Henry Stanley accepted a very difficult chance from a full-blooded drive to mid-on when MacLaren's score was a mere 262. Stanley was, incidentally, the only fielder apart from the wicket-keeper who was not called upon to bowl. The only other chance offered was off the bowling of Lionel Palairet when Archie's score was past the 400 mark; a vicious straight drive failed to make contact with the bowler's hand due more to Palairet's discretion than to his valour.

Lancashire went on to total 801 in eight hours and duly won by an innings and 452 runs. In case it should be thought that Somerset did not warrant first-class status at this time, it may be worth noting that they finished the season by beating Sussex, Kent, Surrey, Yorkshire and Gloucestershire in successive matches. The composition of the team varied considerably, however, and on this occasion it consisted of a cross-section of nine amateurs including a doctor and a vicar. Of the nine bowlers tried, Lionel Palairet's lobs were most successful with four for 133, although Edwin Tyler was to take ten for 49 against Surrey only a few weeks later. An amazing and little known fact about the innings is that the Somerset bowlers averaged twenty-eight five-ball overs per hour throughout – perhaps the chief reason why nobody will ever score 424 in a three-day county match today.

The more one considers this innings, the more incredible it seems. It remained the record score until 1923 when Ponsford scored 429, and it is still the record in England as well as being 60 runs more than any other Englishman has ever scored anywhere.

Two of the Somerset fielders have handed down their impressions of Archie's greatest innings. R. B. Porch remembered in the *Cricketer*: 'MacLaren's stance at the wicket as the ball was delivered was majestic. All he did was done in the grand style. The end of his bat was pointing straight at the sky above his head and his hands were about level with his right shoulder. I do not suppose that absolutely every stroke started like that but that was the main impression...Let the bowler pitch the ball where he liked there would be an unhurried stroke with a full swing to counter it.' S. M. J. Woods, who had considerably more bowling to do against MacLaren, said simply, 'I thought that day would never end. I must have run miles.'

Perhaps the happiest man amongst the one thousand spectators who saw the three days' play was Archie's father who scored in his own book every one of the 424 runs made by his son.

Considering that this monumental innings was made in an era when run scoring on the scale of Bradman and Ponsford had not been dreamed of, the cricketing press took the achievement remarkably in its stride. Today Archie's precarious financial position would have been made secure from the advertising revenue alone, but in the summer of 1895 the great deeds of W.G. somewhat overshadowed those of young Archie. But history was to show that this season, and in particular the feats of Grace and MacLaren, symbolised the coming of the new age in cricket. This age was more than just a golden one, it was the coming to maturity of the game of cricket after more than two centuries of development.

It may sound an over-simplification to define the Golden Age as beginning in 1895, but several cricket historians – notably Patrick Morrah and Rowland Bowen – have pointed out the justification for this statement. Apart from Grace and MacLaren this season saw the enlargement of the County Championship, the debut of Johnny Tyldesley, the first regular season for Ranjitsinhji and the unprecedented feat by Tom Richardson of taking 290 wickets. This latter achievement also helps to indicate that it was not just a Golden Age for batsmen, although the season did see the creation of many new high scoring records amongst the counties.

Although the most astonishing of these events was undoubtedly W.G.'s achievement, it is true to say that MacLaren was the first of the great batsmen to take up his example. During the next decade he was to be closely followed by Ranji, Fry, Jackson, Poore, Tyldesley, Spooner and a host of others, plus the notable Australians, Hill and Trumper.

The perspective in which MacLaren's 424 should be viewed is established by a consideration of the six subsequent occasions on which 400 has been surpassed in first-class cricket (Table 1). It took twenty-eight years before Ponsford showed that the record could be broken and since that occasion a variety of players have periodically followed suit. The post-war examples have been

Table 1 *Quadruple Centuries in First Class Cricket*

	Year	*Score*	*Match*	*Time* (Mins)	*Age*
A. C. MacLaren	1895	424	Lancs v. Somerset	470	23
W. H. Ponsford	1923	429	Victoria v. Tasmania	477	22
W. H. Ponsford	1927	437	Victoria v. Queensland	621	26
D. G. Bradman	1930	452*	NSW v. Queensland	415	21
B.B. Nimbalkar	1948	443*	Maharashtra v. Western Indian States	494	28
Hanif Mohammed	1959	499	Karachi v. Bahawalpur	635	24
Aftab Baloch	1974	428	Sind v. Baluchistan	584	20

confined to the Indian sub-continent where standards of play are sometimes hard to assess, but between the wars Ponsford and Bradman three times bettered MacLaren's score in a seven-year period of gargantuan run scoring. MacLaren's innings was unlike the others in several respects. First, it was played in England where conditions invariably dictate lower scoring, and secondly it was played in a three-day match. In addition, the fact that it was the first such score makes it particularly noteworthy. A suitable analogy might be found in track athletics, where the four-minute-mile barrier seemed impenetrable until Roger Bannister proved that it could be done and was soon followed by many others. This is not intended as an argument that MacLaren's innings was better than the others, but simply that in the context of the different cricket eras concerned it was far more remarkable.

One common factor regarding these quadruple centuries is that, perhaps unsurprisingly, they were all amassed by relatively young men. Not only were skill and opportunity needed but also sheer physical fitness and powers of endurance.

Archie continued to play in most of Lancashire's remaining matches that season, but although he was in obvious good form, he seemed to lose concentration once he had played himself in. In the very next game, against Gloucestershire, he rattled up 25 in half an hour before getting himself out, but later in the match he had to leave the field twice because of cramp and was unable to bat in the second innings. The tremendous physical and mental effort of the record score had obviously taken a heavier toll than was at first apparent.

For the next few games MacLaren continued in irresistible form but could only manage scores of 30 or 40 before losing concentration. It was only a matter of time, though, before he rediscovered the incentive to build a long innings and typically his appetite for runs was re-awakened by adverse batting conditions. A good deal of heavy rain in August meant that in the closing weeks of the season batsmen were for the most part struggling on wet wickets. At the Oval Lancashire were sent in to bat on one such pitch with very little hope of success against a Surrey attack consisting of Lohmann, Richardson, Lockwood, Brockwell and Hayward. On the treacherous turf that day these five were virtually unplayable and the Lancashire batsmen could scarcely lay a bat on their kicking deliveries. None that is except MacLaren, who somehow conjured 52 miraculous runs that earned him more plaudits from those present than even his record score of 424. Certainly this half-century was more than enough for Mold and Briggs to win the match for Lancashire.

As so often happened during MacLaren's career, the sight of the ball popping and turning had brought out the very best in his technique, application and indeed captaincy. For not only was his batting pre-eminent in such conditions, the subtleties of his strategy in the field made all the difference in many a low scoring encounter.

This damp and dreary month of August closed with a series of three matches all of which were completely dominated by MacLaren. Lancashire won all three comfortably, a late charge which all but enabled them to catch the eventual champions, Surrey. Nottinghamshire provided the opposition for the first of this trio of successes on a slow Old Trafford wicket. They batted first and struggled to 154. Thanks to Archie, Lancashire almost passed this total in the last two hours of the day's play. Coming in at 38 for two, MacLaren was 62 not out at close of play. Next day he played a true captain's innings, concentrating his efforts on building an unassailable lead, so that after more than four hours at the wicket his personal tally was 152. The bowlers finished the job for a ten-wicket victory.

In the next game, against Middlesex at Lord's, Archie won the toss and again placed himself at number four in the order. Rain, which delayed the start until two o'clock, ensured that no batsman was going to last long so MacLaren decided on attack, striking out at anything within reach. So successful was his assault that he reached 108 in two hours and provided his team with a respectable total of 260. Just how respectable was shown when Mold and the other Lancashire bowlers summarily dismissed Middlesex for scores of 83 and 77 on the drying wicket.

From London the team travelled up to Leicester for their final game of the season and here met yet another type of wicket. This time the batsmen were confronted with a fast, fiery pitch, completely different from the previous two but equally as difficult. By this time Archie was probably despairing of finding a typical August pitch but he opened the innings and effortlessly dismissed the Leicestershire bowlers to all parts. In just two and a quarter hours he made 135 out of 220 including a century before lunch and this was more than enough to ensure an easy win.

In each of these three matches Archie had been so successful that he did not have to bat in a second innings, thereby reaching the notable achievement of three consecutive centuries within the space of a week. More significantly these innings were played on three different kinds of wicket which, taken together, posed all the questions that can be asked of a batsman. The promising novice had this season attained the distinction of an established master. This final surge by Archie also enabled him to overtake W. G. Grace at the top of the national averages, a duel which excited considerable speculation at the time. (MacLaren, with an average of 51.21, was strictly speaking second to L. H. Gwynn but the latter played only ten innings.) This achievement meant much to MacLaren, not because of a thirst for records but because he had revered W.G. since childhood and was in Gilbert Jessop's words 'a great favourite of the G.O.M.'s'.

During the ensuing winter the Lancashire committee were only too pleased to mark Archie's great deeds this season and they duly elected him a life member of the club in January. The annual dinner at the Albion Hotel, Manchester, was also centred around him and he was presented with a gold watch and chain to commemorate his performances.

As one final thought on this 'annus mirabilis' is it too romantic to suppose that Archie's future wife, who had so turned his head during the Australian tour, was in some way partly responsible for the tremendous success since then? In the space of just six months since their meeting he had scored a century for England against Australia, amassed a world record 424 and made three successive centuries.

4
The Sydney Wizard

After the glorious successes of 1895 the following season began with MacLaren unavailable again until July. Remarkable as it seems, when he did return to the cricket field his first two games were no less than the Gentlemen v. Players match at Lord's and the second Test match against the touring Australians. Despite his lack of practice the first of these matches saw Archie start confidently enough with 42 in a six-wicket win for the amateurs. Encouraged by this performance and fully aware of the local interest that would be generated, the Lancashire committee then took the bold step of selecting MacLaren for the forthcoming Test at Old Trafford, his first in England. At that time the national side was selected by the county committee on whose ground the Test was to take place.

The first game of the series, at Lord's, had been won by England thanks to Tom Richardson and George Lohmann who had shot out Australia in just seventy-five minutes on the first morning. All the same, for the second Test three team changes were made, the Manchester authorities going along with the majority of public opinion and selecting Ranjitsinhji for his debut after the Indian Prince had been considered ineligible at Lord's. The choice of MacLaren, with only one first-class innings behind him, was a surprising selection although he was, on reputation, undoubtedly worth a place in England's best XI. Throughout this series the selection of the team produced its usual controversies and arguments; William Gunn, who had not originally been selected for this match after appearing at Lord's, was asked to play at the eleventh hour but refused the honour.

The game itself provided a good win for Australia. They scored 412, a heroic Richardson taking seven for 168, and then forced England to follow on despite resistance from Ranji and Lilley. MacLaren, making his first Test appearance in England and before his own Manchester crowd, could not have fared worse. He was out to his very first ball, the victim of a juggling catch off the bowling of Tom McKibbin. The gamble of playing a man out of practice had failed, and the only excuse that could be offered was that MacLaren was suffering from a very constricting stiff neck.

The remainder of the match has since become one of the more heroic pages of cricket's history for the way in which Ranji fought a lone battle in the second innings to give the lion-hearted Tom Richardson a total, however paltry, to bowl at. Sir Neville Cardus' graphic and moving reconstruction of how the Surrey fast bowler toiled through forty-two overs before Australia struggled to 125 for seven and victory is rightly regarded as one of his finest essays. Writing in the *Cricketer* twenty-five years later MacLaren recalled that Harry Trott, the Australian captain, found this last innings so nerve-racking that he had to leave the ground and drive round Manchester in a cab until the match was decided.

After the disappointment of the Test Archie eventually made his first appearance for Lancashire in the Roses match on 20 July. Taking over the captaincy of the side he managed to show some good batting form with scores of 32 and 31 out of two miserable totals, but the result was a bad defeat for the county. This game was followed by a most controversial meeting with W. G. Grace's Gloucestershire side at Old Trafford. After winning the toss MacLaren opened the batting and had scored only 2 when he played a ball from Charles Townsend to square leg and set off for a run. Quick as a flash W.G. noticed that a bail had been dislodged by Archie's foot and immediately shouted, 'You're out Archie! Chuck her up!' MacLaren simply carried on running and shouted back that he had completed his stroke and therefore was not out, a view endorsed by the umpire. W.G. was furious but the umpire, Arthur Shrewsbury's brother, William, was determined not to be browbeaten by the Old Man and stuck to what most spectators thought was a correct decision.

In Appendix A MacLaren gives his own account of this incident which was described by one newspaper as follows: 'W.G. fumed and gesticulated worse than any old chronic Militia Colonel on parade, and when MacLaren came across to show that he kicked the bail off when starting to run, the amiable giant would neither be convinced nor remain quiet. Thus the game was suspended for some minutes while the onlookers volumed forth, "Umpire, Umpire!".' Archie eventually took his score to 56, apparently unaffected by W.G.'s sulking and displays of temper which persisted throughout the innings. Even at the end of the day, when Gloucestershire had to bat in failing light, he was heard to say, 'I'll tell young Archie something when he comes in'. To make matters worse one of the Lancashire members passed a remark to W.G. as he came off at lunchtime, and the Gloucestershire captain insisted that the man be censured by the committee. In his reminiscences Jessop informs us that W.G.'s team-mates were afraid to speak to him or catch his eye for the rest of the day.

This lively episode at Old Trafford was followed by Archie's first ever appearance in the Canterbury week, held at the beginning of August. Late on the second evening of the match Lancashire's hopes looked slim as they began the follow on 148 in arrears. MacLaren, though, was not going to give up without a fight and he set his sights on playing out the final day and denying Kent the points. This he managed almost single-handed, scoring an undefeated 226 out of the total of 393 for six, Johnny Tyldesley's 51 being the next best score. He hit thirty-four boundaries, mainly drives, and forsook his usual carefree style for 'correct cricket'. Yet 393 in six hours ten minutes seems, in these more sober times, an enterprising way of playing out time for a draw.

This fine innings persuaded the Surrey committee that Archie was in the sort of form to avenge his Old Trafford failures in the third and final Test at the Oval. The ramifications leading to the final composition of the England team are shrouded in uncertainty. The professionals Lohmann, Richardson, Abel, Hayward and Gunn at first refused to take part unless the usual fee of £10 was doubled, and when that was sorted out the controversy of back-hander payments for amateurs reared its head. Stoddart and W.G. were the targets for abuse in the press, although MacLaren was surprisingly ignored. Ultimately the overworked Surrey secretary, C. W. Alcock, issued a statement detailing the expenses paid to W.G. who duly took his place at the head of the team. A. E. Stoddart, however, withdrew from the team, officially because of the effects of a heavy cold, although Stoddart's biographer, David Frith, concludes that the Middlesex player was a little more sensitive to 'vilification' in the press than was the durable W.G. Writing twenty-five years later MacLaren chose to interpret Stoddart's withdrawal as a generous gesture which allowed him a place in the side, but the real reasons were doubtless more personal.

The match itself had been keenly awaited by the public since the result of the series was still in the balance. Eventually England secured the Ashes, winning a low-scoring battle on an increasingly spiteful, wet wicket mainly by virtue of putting 114 for three on the board by the close of day one. Archie's share was a valuable 20 during the course of which he raised the hundred with a huge straight drive into the pavilion, but on the Friday morning he was dismissed straightaway by Hughie Trumble who revelled in the helpful conditions. The newspaper reporters of those days were considerably more lyrical than their counterparts today and apparently, 'the ball with which the long Victorian beat MacLaren was a perfect marvel, pitched very wide of the off-stump and upset the piece of timber nearest to MacLaren's leg.' In the second innings he 'played forward to Jones but failed to allow for a two-foot break', with his score on 6. The target of 111 was beyond the Australians, who succumbed to the unplayable J. T. Hearne and Bobby Peel for only 44 runs. A notable feature of the game seems to have been the brilliant fielding of both teams, but 'even in such select company, Mr MacLaren shone conspicuously', and 'England fielded well, MacLaren being the shining light'.

The day after the Test Archie hurried up from London to Manchester in order to lead Lancashire against Derbyshire. Arriving at Old Trafford shortly after the start of the game, as arranged, he found that the substitute fielder, Frank Ward, had been inadvertently called up to bowl, so there was no way in which MacLaren could play. It is unfortunately not on record what his comments were to the vice-captain.

For the remainder of the season Archie scored consistently well to finish top of the Lancashire averages with 713 runs at 54.85 per innings. Perhaps if he could have played in more than ten matches the county may even have improved on their position as runners up to Yorkshire in the championship. A contemporary newspaper commented, 'Such magnificent batting as shown by the Old Harrovian during this latter part of the season has been quite one of its features.' The *Globe* supported this with 'There was nothing more remarkable in recent cricket than A. C. MacLaren's batting.'

What then was Archie's standing at this stage of his career? Despite his lack of success in this season's Tests he was now generally regarded by the public as one of the leading batsmen of the day, and he was even interviewed in the *Strand Magazine*. The record-breaking feats of the previous year had been consolidated and, at the age of twenty-four, he was at his athletic peak. He batted with a sureness and authority which gave the impression during a big innings that he would never get out. The only cloud on the horizon was that his shaky finances meant that he had to sit on the sidelines for the first half of the season, a state of affairs which, although frustrating, never seemed to affect his form. In fact this limitation may have provided the freshness and incentive to continue his innings well beyond the hundred mark. Certainly the long grind of playing non-stop throughout the season in later years produced a tendency to hit out frantically for a dazzling 30 or 40.

Even in these early years, however, Archie did far more than simply destroy bowling when the conditions favoured batting; he also had a reputation for succeeding when the odds were against him. At the close of this season of 1896 one commentator noted, 'The best proof of his exceptional ability can be found in the fact that he is capable of making good scores on all sorts of wickets.' The Cardus picture, thoroughly deserved and accurate, of the 'Grand Manner' and 'dismissing the ball from his presence' tends to obscure his ability as an obdurate fighter. Some years ago Rowland Bowen attempted a statistical assessment of the match-decisiveness of an innings, and MacLaren surely played a greater proportion of these than most players. A typical example was furnished in this season of 1896 in the match against Surrey. On a real old fashioned 'sticky' wicket Lancashire at 30 for six were finding the meagre total of 60 which was required for victory rather beyond them. Just as he had done the previous year against Lohmann and Richardson, MacLaren steered his team home again, this time with an undefeated 32 out of 60 for six. This innings, small though it seems, was priceless to his team.

The pattern set over the last two years, teaching until late July and then bursting onto the cricket scene, was to be repeated until the close of the century. Archie was never one for practice so he could easily come into the side and score runs straightaway. If he hit a bad patch he would simply put himself down the order, sometimes as low as nine, until he was back in form. Even MacLaren's self-assurance was severely tested, however, when he made his re-appearance against Sussex on 15 July 1897. Not only did he twice drop Ranji in the course of the Sussex innings but his captaincy was roundly criticised. He kept Johnny Briggs bowling over after over despite tremendous punishment, and the situation became so farcical that the crowd cheered every time the luckless bowler walked up to the crease at the start of an over. MacLaren's reaction was to display his worst qualities of pig-headedness and superiority by keeping Briggs on. One newspaper commented, 'To the jollying of the crowd he was as impervious as a stone wall; ironical cheering whenever he fielded a ball had no effect. Altogether the affair resolved itself into a demonstration of cheap dignity on the part of the Lancashire captain in which he was the solitary loser.' Another referred to him as 'Haughty Archibald'.

MacLaren might almost have wished he had kept to his original intention of not playing any cricket at all that summer. Stoddart was taking out another team to Australia during the coming winter and Archie had planned to marry the girl he had met three years previously. To this end he was going straight out to Melbourne in August, but eventually the plan was changed. Although he managed to play out the season for Lancashire, he asked to be relieved of the captaincy and the job reverted once more to A. N. Hornby who was now aged fifty and as club president must have thought his playing days were over.

After the traumatic game against Sussex Archie answered his critics with a sustained burst of run scoring. In the next match, the Roses encounter at Bradford, he scored 152 in only three hours and this was followed by a rumbustious 70 against Somerset during which his old friends, Tyler and Woods, were smashed to all parts. There followed an equally rapid 68 at Gloucestershire. Then, in August, came Archie's second visit to the Canterbury festival, where the Kent bowlers were given another opportunity to study his method. No doubt they considered that his masterful 244 on top of the previous year's 226 not out was just a little too much of a good thing. This magnificent innings, which ended towards the close of a first day on which Lancashire totalled 390 for nine, lasted for five hours. The Kent bowlers managed to curb his powerful off-drives but he showed his all-round skill with innumerable on-drives, powerful cuts and his own inimitable hook stroke which produced most of his thirty-eight boundaries.

At this time Archie's marvellous form was the highlight of the season, and after his late start he had now scored 596 runs at an average of 99.22. Most of these innings were being watched at the other end by his England colleague and opening partner, Albert Ward. A great batsman in his own right and a tremendous servant to Lancashire, Ward was repeatedly reported as scoring at half the rate of his partner but his unselfish and experienced support were invaluable.

Inspired by MacLaren's late charge, the Red Rose county pulled off the championship for the first time since 1881. They had been runners up five times in the seven years since Archie's debut, but this season the bowling resources were completed by the discovery

of Cuttell and Hallam. The season closed on a pleasant note as
A. N. Hornby presented Archie with a spirit tantalus from the club
to mark his forthcoming wedding.

It was, therefore, a buoyant, super-confident MacLaren who set
out for Australia to show that he was the equal of any batsman in
the world. He must have hoped that his marriage in March would
be the crowning glory of a victorious and successful tour, but
unfortunately from the team's point of view this was not to be.
Many misfortunes befell the party, not least the death in England
of Stoddart's mother and the captain's subsequent melancholic
withdrawal.

Throughout the tour MacLaren's personal batting form was
nothing short of brilliant. Although the series was lost by four
matches to one, MacLaren and Ranji broke a series of records to
place themselves clearly at the head of England's batting. The spotlight fell mainly on the Indian Prince, who was making his only
tour to Australia, and despite a terrible succession of illnesses he
did not disappoint the thousands who came to see him. But the
efforts of these two batsmen were not enough to offset the absence
of the stalwarts of the previous tour—Ward, Brown and Peel. The
new blood which Stoddart included at their expense was far from successful; Hirst, Mason and Wainwright proved most disappointing.

The team started in fine form, winning two and drawing one of
the three first-class games which preceded the opening Test match.
Archie, who had travelled to Australia two weeks earlier than the
rest of the party, did nothing outstanding in the first two matches.
Doubtless he found the team's visit to the races, including the
Melbourne Cup, more of a high spot. This equine contest, one of
the most famous in the world, was only fitted into the tour itinerary
by the premature curtailment of the South Australia game at
Adelaide, which was left drawn after only a couple of token hours
play on the fourth day.

The third game of the tour, against New South Wales at Sydney,
brought a return to form for Archie. On the second morning, with
the wicket in a lively state, the home team lost their last five first
innings wickets for only 7 runs, to total 311. The huge 31,000

crowd then watched as McKibbin and Coningham repeatedly beat the batsmen, and by lunch the England innings was tottering at 32 for two. Despite these early difficulties Archie managed to hang on, and by the time William Storer came in he was finding the boundary regularly with ringing drives. This pair proceeded to add 146 of which 62 came in a hectic thirteen-minute spell. Eventually Archie perished, as so often, caught in the deep. He had scored 142 out of 250 for five without giving a chance. This display gave Stoddart's team a small first innings lead, and on the fourth day they set out to score 237 for victory. After losing Mason at 12, the great pair, MacLaren and Ranjitsinhji, came together and put on 97 in the hour before lunch. After the interval these two made short work of the target and both scored centuries in an eight-wicket win. During the course of this innings Archie broke two bats with the sheer force of his hitting. This was the first time a batsman had scored two centuries in a match in Australia and the deed was rapturously received by the public and the press alike. This was the first of Archie's succession of marvellous innings at Sydney, after the ground had been strangely unlucky for him in 1894–5 when he managed only 41 runs in six innings. From now on though, his scoring feats were to earn him the nickname 'the Sydney wizard' and he became a great favourite with the local spectators. Nobody who saw any of his innings during this or the next tour would admit that England had ever possessed a finer player. MacLaren loved to tell people that you only had to 'poke your tongue out at the ball' for it to go for four on the perfect wickets at Sydney.

After this great achievement it was soon back to the serious business of studying form and handicapping for an outing to Brisbane races. It was also at Brisbane that Archie produced another awesome display of his maturing powers, against a combined Queensland/New South Wales XIII. Stoddart won the toss for the first time on the tour and by the end of a useful day's practice the score was 333 for four with MacLaren 64 not out having gone in at number five. By 4.45 the following afternoon the total had been increased to a towering 636. In under two and a half hours Archie

(181) and young N. F. Druce (126) had put on no less than 252. Although the match was not ranked first-class, the bowling attack included the Test players McKibbin, Howell and Turner, the 'Terror' of not so many years ago. The game was left drawn. Archie and Stoddart stood down from the next country game in order to go shooting and apparently they narrowly avoided death in an accident on the drive back. A few days later, however, tragedy really did strike with the news that Stoddart's mother, to whom he was devoted, had died in England. The skipper was very badly affected and for him the rest of the tour was a sad chore to be completed as soon as possible. Certainly there was no chance of his playing in the first Test at Sydney, despite a postponement due to heavy rain.

It was in these sad circumstances that MacLaren first assumed the captaincy of his country. On a fine December morning he walked out with Harry Trott to toss for innings on the ground which had recently been the scene of his twin century performance. With this first duty performed successfully, Archie and Mason opened the series on a good wicket opposed by the fiery pace of Ernest Jones and the concealed spin of Tom McKibbin. It was noticeable that the Australian skipper would not bowl Jones from the end at which Jim Phillips was umpiring. Phillips, who was travelling with the English team as umpire and manager, had no-balled 'Jonah' for throwing in the very first match of the tour and was a self-appointed scourge of doubtful actions. In those days, incidentally, it was only the bowler's umpire who could call no-ball.

Fair or not, even Jones' fastest deliveries could not penetrate Archie's defence on such a perfect Sydney wicket as this. After the early dismissal of Mason, Tom Hayward was just as commanding at the other end and 163 was on the board before the second wicket fell. The Australians must have been alarmed to find MacLaren in this mood. Gone was the carefree approach. The responsibility of captaincy and the perfection of the wicket which made risks unnecessary combined to bring a new determination to his play. As Ranji commented, 'His coolness was marvellous, and it was clear to everybody that he meant to make a great effort.' MacLaren's inevitable century was still posted in less than three hours when, after being on 99 for some time, he cut Trumble for four. This was his fourth successive century in important matches, including the non-first-class Brisbane game, and it contained not the semblance of a chance until he was dismissed shortly after tea.

On the second day Ranji, who had been extremely ill with quinsy, virtually secured the game for England with a phenomenally brave innings. He was attended by doctors during each interval and almost collapsed with exhaustion, but he still scored 175 in an England total of 551. By the close of the second day Australia were 80 for five and the game was gone. In the follow on the redoubtable left-handers, Darling and Hill, forced England to bat again, but with only 95 needed MacLaren finished matters in just over an hour with 50 not out. With his score on 5 there had been a loud appeal for caught behind against MacLaren which the umpire ruled not out. Archie did not walk, even though he knew he had hit the ball, but after the game he selected a bat from the dozen or so he carried with him and presented it to the Australian wicket-keeper, Jim Kelly. Even in those days 'walking' was apparently rare in the most crucial Test matches.

Although the second Test followed almost immediately, the balance between the sides had altered radically. The new year was unbearably hot and the winning of the toss was all the powerful young Australian team needed in order to take a vice-like grip on the series; in the face of a huge total England followed on and were beaten by an innings. The wicket broke up badly, forming large cracks which Noble and Trumble exploited perfectly. In his after-match speech MacLaren expressed the hope that future Test wickets would last a little longer, but this was predictably interpreted as sour grapes by the Australian press.

Stoddart again took his place for the third Test, leaving MacLaren to reflect on his two eventful matches as England's captain. He had scored a century, won the first match easily and lost the second heavily. There had been incidents; in one, the Australian spearhead, Jones, was no-balled for throwing and on another

49

occasion profuse apologies had been required when McLeod, who was deaf, left his ground after being bowled by a no-ball which he had not heard called and was run out by Storer. Archie himself had been severely criticised for his refusal to use the bowling of Ted Wainwright and he was several times involved in newspaper controversy during both games. As always MacLaren was attracting incident and discord like a magnet.

The pattern of the third game was identical to that of the previous one, with England following on 295 behind. In the second innings, however, MacLaren fought the Australian bowlers every inch of the way. During over five hours of unrelenting concentration and uncharacteristic defence he scored 124, but still the game was lost by an innings. This was easily the slowest century of Archie's long career, but in its own way it was one of his finest innings. With little chance of saving the game he decided to give nothing and provided further evidence that when necessary he could temper his natural dash with rigorous application. The Australian spectators showed their usual admiration for a fighter, and when he was finally dismissed they were unstinting in their applause.

The fourth match featured England's third successive follow on and the series was lost. In the second innings MacLaren and Ranji were well set at 94 for two when a fly apparently entered Archie's eye just as Trumble bowled, causing him to pop up a catch. Ranji unfortunately claimed in the press that this incident cost England the game and, not surprisingly, MacLaren suffered several days of sarcastic ribbing in print. The final match of the series, in which MacLaren again took over the leadership, exposed once more all the failings of brittle batting and indifferent bowling. Despite a substantial first innings lead and a faultless 'Sydney innings' of 65 from Archie himself, Joe Darling snatched the game for Australia with a dramatic 160. A series of crashing drives off Richardson brought up the South Australian's century in only ninety-one minutes and, to add insult to injury, he was using the bat which MacLaren had given to Kelly after the first Test of the series. In the England second innings Archie's marvellous sequence on this ground ended when he chased the very first ball, which was almost a wide, to be caught at third man. The series also ended on a sad note for Stoddart who hardly endeared himself to the locals by complaining bitterly about the barracking of the crowd.

A resounding failure then but for Archie the runs had never stopped flowing. Immediately before the last Test, in the return match with New South Wales at Sydney, a world record aggregate of 1,739 runs had been scored. Archie wrenched his ankle fielding and could only bat number nine in the first innings. Nevertheless he hit up a rapid 61 before he was bowled by one of Noble's away-swinging off-spinners. After a feast of run-making Stoddart's team were eventually set a massive 603 to win but at the close of the fifth day even this appeared possible at 258 for one. MacLaren was undefeated on 135 with Ranji his partner at 42. The answer to their onslaught was for the home team to open the attack next morning with Donnan, primarily a batsman who seldom bowled. The thinking behind this ploy soon became apparent when he began to bowl round the wicket with an exaggerated follow through down the middle of the pitch. Whether deliberate or not the effect was to tear up the turf and to destroy the batsmen's concentration. Both Ranji and MacLaren were out by the time 13 runs had been added, and it was not until Hirst and Hayward were batting that some objection was made to Donnan's actions. The team never recovered and were easily beaten by 239 runs. MacLaren was livid. As captain he lodged an official complaint with the New South Wales authorities, making it clear that he saw Donnan's bowling as a premeditated tactic. Unfortunately for Archie his protest backfired when the New South Wales Association took umbrage and rescinded the fifty guineas wedding present that they had promised MacLaren and his future wife.

The wedding took place at Toorak, a suburb of Melbourne, on 17 March, St Patrick's Day (Maud and Archie both had Irish blood). The English had just beaten Victoria at the end of the tour. Archie's bride was Kathleen Maud Power, the second daughter of Robert Power, the Irish born and now extremely wealthy director of the Dalgety pastoral empire and one of the founders of the

Victoria Racing Club. As well as having a passion for horse racing Mr Power had himself played cricket for Victoria in 1858, so there was considerable common ground between Archie and his father-in-law. Maud, as she preferred to be called, was two years older than Archie, short in stature and very beautiful with her tightly curled auburn hair. She was artistic in nature, being interested in music, and was noted for her fine singing voice.

The wedding was a highlight of the social calendar and the local gossip columns were full of the event. The combination of handsome England cricket captain and wealthy landowner's daughter was too good to miss. Sir Arthur Priestley, who was travelling with the team, acted as best man and the Rev. Canon Tucker officiated. Miss Millie Carter thoughtfully decorated the altar and church with floral wickets, bats and balls, while the bridesmaids wore the red rose of Lancashire and bouquets in the Stoddart team colours. All the touring team were in attendance and on the appointed day it seemed that everyone in Melbourne wanted to see the couple married. Before the ceremony the 'irreverent and indecent crowd' surged into the church, taking every possible vantage point including the pulpit. During the service the Rev. Tucker twice had to admonish the congregation for standing on pews and chattering. In the words of one society column, 'The sanctity of the holy house was for the nonce forgotten.'

When the ceremony was over the onlookers charged all over the church, tearing down the decorations in an effort to secure the exquisitely made floral souvenirs. After all this excitement Archie and his bride went to Governor and Lady Brassey's vice-regal hill residence of Healesville for a brief honeymoon before rejoining the other cricketers at Port Adelaide for the voyage home aboard the *Ormuz*.

5

In the Footsteps of W.G.

Returning from Australia with Maud, Archie had too many distractions to concentrate on cricket. As well as setting up home in a delightful old country mansion in Wokingham, he had to continue his teaching until July and for the rest of the summer was plagued by bouts of ill health and injury. Although the young couple had received a handsome cheque as a wedding present from the Power family, this had to be spent on the house, so MacLaren's financial future was far from solved.

During the winter tour Archie had promised Ted Wainwright that he would be able to make his seasonal debut in the Yorkshire professionals' benefit match on 11 July. Unfortunately the funeral of I. D. Walker, Archie's old instructor and friend from Harrow, forced a change of plan and it was not until the following week that he could set foot on the cricket field.

As had been the case two years previously, this first match was one of the highlights of the cricketing calendar—Gentlemen v. Players at Lord's. In this season of 1898, though, the historic fixture was even more important than usual since it celebrated W. G. Grace's Golden Jubilee. The start of the match was put back a week so that it could coincide with the Grand Old Man's fiftieth birthday. Archie was delighted that he could play: in fact the team photo of the Gentlemen was one of his most prized possessions and always had a place of honour in Archie's many different homes over the years.

The match itself was a gripping struggle with W.G. the leading figure. The Players were in a strong position after their first innings of 335 had been followed by rain which completely altered the previously passive wicket. Still the Gentlemen fell only 32 short of this total, thanks in part to Archie who top-scored with a brilliant 50 in his first innings of the season. After the professionals had made defeat an impossibility, the Gentlemen were left with three hours to bat out, a task which seemed beyond them at 77 for seven. At this point W.G., who was lame and had a bad hand, came to the wicket only to see two more wickets fall at 80. The game looked all over when last man Kortright joined his skipper, but in a little over an hour the pair raised the score by 78 and a draw appeared possible. It is history now how Lockwood returned to the attack for a last desperate fling and succeeded in removing Kortright with two minutes left for play, but nobody could deny that this was W.G.'s moment.

After the great match it was not until August that MacLaren made a belated re-appearance for Lancashire at his favourite Canterbury ground. Although the Kent bowlers were pleased to see him go for 39 in the first innings, he kept up his marvellous record on the last day with 76 in ninety-five minutes. He managed only another five matches that August before an attack of neuralgia at Lord's kept him out for the remainder of the season, and Lancashire finished a disappointing sixth. Injuries to their key bowlers and the absence of MacLaren had destroyed any hopes of another championship win.

After this virtually blank summer Archie looked forward to the last season of the old century with mixed feelings. Although he would be renewing old friendships with the touring Australians, his duties at school would again foreshorten his cricket. In spite of this Lancashire were keen that he should resume the captaincy whenever possible so he was appointed joint leader with G. R. Bardswell.

The predominant subjects of interest were of course the touring team and how England would fare in the Test series. Most commentators, including Archie, were enthusiastic about the Australians who were widely expected to repeat the treatment meted out to Stoddart's last combination. Although England would now be able to call on Fry, Jackson and the ageing W.G., they were to be desperately short of a spearhead bowler. Tom Richardson was at last showing signs of the terrible wear and tear he had been subjected to over the last six years, and the only comparable bowler, W. H. Lockwood, suffered from injury early in the season. He did recover to such an extent that he performed the double, but the vast majority of his wickets were taken late in the season and he only played in the final Test of the summer.

MacLaren could only watch as the tourists flexed their muscles against the counties, and he had still not lifted a bat in anger when England stumbled to a draw in the first game at Trent Bridge. Nobody had previously doubted England's batting which was strong enough on paper to have Tyldesley at seven and Hirst at nine, but the Australian bowling quartet of Jones, Howell, Noble and Trumble had gained an important advantage.

The general uneasiness caused by this poor performance was reflected in the actions of the selection committee who met at the Sports Club the week before the Lord's Test, the highlight of the year. This season was the first in which the MCC took on the selection of England teams, formerly the duty of the county on whose ground the game was to be played. The committee consisted of W. G. Grace, Lord Hawke and H. W. Bainbridge and they had the power to co-opt two amateurs out of the first six chosen, in fact F. S. Jackson and C. B. Fry. Their first job was to improve the bowling, but their efforts smacked rather of panic. J. T. Hearne was dropped and three players new to Test cricket were included—C. L. Townsend, W. Mead and G. L. Jessop. These were all in good form in county matches and with Richardson, Lockwood, Mold and Kortright all unavailable perhaps little else could be done. In addition the wicket-keeper was changed, Lilley instead of Storer.

The other point on the committee's agenda was the position of W. G. Grace, England's captain in the first Test. Although still no worse with the bat than many of his younger colleagues, he had expressed a wish to drop out because of the embarrassment he felt regarding his slowness in the field and between the wickets. The suggested replacement, as batsman and captain, was MacLaren. Even though he had not played a single match yet that season this had not affected his form over the last four years, and it was felt that his experience in Australia made him the man for the job. The committee was split, though, and deadlock had been reached when, according to his own account, C. B. Fry strode into the meeting, late. He was apparently asked by W.G. whether MacLaren should play at Lord's and it was only after he had enthusiastically approved that he was told that W.G. would be the one omitted. When the side was announced in the press, with the statement that a captain would not be appointed until the morning of the match, it was harshly received. In the event the decision on the captaincy was revealed a couple of days before the game, and Archie received a telegram from W.G. informing him that the job was his. It has occasionally been suggested in retrospect that the captaincy should have passed to F. S. Jackson on seniority. This was hardly likely at the time, though, as Archie already had considerable experience of captaining Lancashire, and indeed England on the last tour. Jackson was not an established leader in the eyes of the public due to the immovable presence of Lord Hawke in the Yorkshire side.

So to Lord's, where the result was a humiliating ten-wicket defeat for the drastically reshaped England team. The bowling which everyone had doubted was exposed by the brilliant batting of Hill and Trumper who each made 135. The MacLaren luck was out, as so often and Jessop strained his back so badly that he could only bowl at half pace for the rest of the season. The batting, which contained some of the greatest names of the Golden Age, had been taken for granted, but the fearsome Ernest Jones bowled 72.1 overs in the match to take ten for 164.

What of MacLaren in this fiasco? On the first morning he won the toss and there followed a buzz of excitement as he strode out to the wicket to open the batting. It did not matter that he had not played a single innings that season, he was captain of England and he would go in first. Unfortunately this brave gesture proved a failure, the tremendous pace of Jones bowling him neck and crop for only 4. As the newspaper *Cricket* commented, 'The number of ''I told you so's'' which passed round the ground could almost be calculated.' A collapse followed which was only partially arrested by Jackson and the debutant Jessop who scored a promising 51 in sixty-seven minutes.

After Australia had amassed a lead of 215 it was confidently expected that England would be able to see out the last day for a draw, but again there was a collapse to 94 for four. MacLaren had demoted himself to number six and one can only wonder at his thoughts as he marched out to join Hayward who had so far stood alone against Jones. All we know is that he played what everyone present described as his greatest innings, 88 not out in a miserable total of 240. In averting the innings defeat and playing with such mastery for just under two and a half hours, he redeemed his own selection even if he could not save the match. The contemporary verdict was that his innings outshone even those of Hill and Trumper, and both Warner and Jessop went on record as considering it the highlight of his career – a considerable claim.

Between the second and third Tests MacLaren afforded himself the luxury of his first two games of the season for Lancashire, making an immediate impact. Against his favourite enemy, Yorkshire, on a bowler's wicket, he scored a chanceless 126 out of a total of only 203. Hirst, Haigh and Rhodes were the ideal exploiters of such a wicket and the next highest score was only 18. *Cricket* described the innings as 'an altogether remarkable display' and the bowling of Briggs and Mold was enough to win the game by 59 runs. During the last innings when the game was delicately poised, play was interrupted on several occasions while Lord Hawke came onto the field for discussions with MacLaren. It transpired that this was due to the selection of the England team for the third Test at Leeds, which was confused by the kind of uncertainty that seems so strange to us today but was almost commonplace about this period. Amazingly, F. S. Jackson and Arthur Shrewsbury were both selected but declined to play. Shrewsbury, forty-three years of age but batting as well as ever, stated that the strain of playing a Test at his time of life was too great. Jackson, despite much public rumour to the effect that he was jealous of MacLaren being captain, would only say that his reasons were private. Jackson had also refused to play against MacLaren in the recent Roses game which had ended Yorkshire's championship hopes and press criticism was harsh. Amongst other comments were: 'An unfortunate incident in connection with the Test match was the little display of pique on the part of F. S. Jackson' – 'Jackson's outward show of vexation' – 'Jackson is undoubtedly MacLaren's senior in first-class cricket but A. C. MacLaren is the better captain'. In the end Jackson was prevailed upon to play although he contributed little.

The match itself was ruined by rain, the whole of the last day being lost, but England would probably have clinched victory inside two days, except for the loss of Lancashire's popular Johnny Briggs after the Australian first innings. Having bowled well to take three for 53 in thirty overs on the first day, he was seized by an epileptic fit that evening at the Empire Music Hall in Leeds and was removed to an asylum where he continued to have seizures all night. Although the greatest tragedy was Briggs' (he died in 1902), the loss of his bowling on the second afternoon meant that Australia held on against second-string bowlers, thereby saving the game. This match provided further justification for MacLaren's reputation as an unlucky captain in Test cricket. He had been brought in as captain on a hiding to nothing and after the defeat at Lord's had been mainly responsible for reshaping the team. He had urged the introduction of 'Sailor' Young on the grounds that he would dismiss the left-handers Darling and Hill, which he did, and the choice of Briggs looked like being just as successful until the terrible illness struck. With any luck at all Archie would have been responsible for leading England right back into the series.

Before the next tussle with Australia Archie managed his third game for Lancashire and also appeared for the Gentlemen v. Players, W. G. Grace's last appearance in this fixture at Lord's. Although Archie batted in good style without making a large score it was his athletic fielding that caught the attention. Stationed at deep square leg for the lob bowling of D. L. A. Jephson, he caught

Trott and Hirst with magnificent running catches. Hirst's powerful pull never rose more than fifteen feet off the ground, Archie
taking the ball at knee height with arms outstretched whilst sprint-
ing at full speed. Even old W.G. rushed right out to the boundary to
shake MacLaren by the hand.

The fourth Test was drawn very much in England's favour,
Australia being forced to follow on. The tourists were extricated
from defeat by two innings from Monty Noble which deserve to be
ranked with the more famous match-saving efforts—not that he
was attractive to watch, batting a total of nine and a half hours for
60 not out and 89. The match may well have been won had Lilley
not missed a couple of catches, but it was not revealed until later
that he was keeping wicket with a broken finger. Despite this, the
general view was that the good work started at Leeds had been
continued, and England were now carrying the attack to
Australia. At last they seemed to possess a fast bowling spearhead
in Bradley of Kent who took five for 67 in the first innings,
although he never became the permanent replacement that was
needed for Tom Richardson.

Archie was absent from cricket for a fortnight after the Test but
again showed no lack of form when he returned for the Roses game
at Old Trafford, scoring 116 in 160 minutes. There was, incidentally, a touch of generosity on the last day of this drawn game,
rather uncharacteristic of these normally dour affairs. With only
time for one more over before close of play MacLaren himself
bowled a series of full pitches to leg, thereby enabling David
Denton to take his score from 89 to 101 not out.

The last Test, at the Oval, was a certain draw on a perfect batting
wicket which saw England score 435 for four on the first day. The
Golden Age was displayed as never before with Jackson scoring 95
before lunch and Fry and MacLaren adding 110 in seventy
minutes. Although Lockwood bowled miraculously on the
unresponsive pitch to force Australia to follow on, there was never
any chance of a result in three days. Indeed this season was the
cause of much discussion as to whether Tests should be played to a
finish in this country, an argument which MacLaren supported

fervently. In fact, Test match duration in England was not even increased to four days until 1930.

The summer of 1899 ended, then, with English cricket and the status of A. C. MacLaren in a much healthier position than had been gloomily forecast in early July. The Australians had been hailed as world-beaters and the selection of the English team at Lord's had been scorned as sheer panic. Almost every contemporary publication managed to find an article on 'The decay of English cricket'. In the end, although the series was lost, England had turned the corner and made the Australians struggle in each of the last three matches. A feeling of moral victory at its most satisfying was prevalent.

It was probably about this time that the importance of captaincy first began to be fully recognised. Perhaps it is just that 'in-depth' reporting of the games and personalities increased then, but there is a feeling that before Trott, Darling and MacLaren the captain did not have the same pre-occupation with tactics, field settings and so on. Certainly Trott and Darling had a profound influence not only on the long line of astute Australian skippers which followed, but also on MacLaren. The cream of English amateur batting had frequently failed in Test matches and much of the credit must go to Joe Darling. He ensured that his bowlers used their heads and seldom fed a batsman's favourite shot, as often happened in county cricket. Also Ernest Jones, realising that Fry, Ranji and company were no happier against fast short balls than are the present generation, used them repeatedly and with every justification.

The season had been a disappointing one for Lancashire who were without a regular captain, the only glimmer of light being the debut of Reggie Spooner. He was soon to take his place as one of the greatest of stylists and his name is forever linked with MacLaren's. This season he scored 69 and 198 for Marlborough against Rugby at Lord's and followed with 158 for the Lancashire second XI. In his debut for the county, against Middlesex at headquarters, the boy batted like a master against Albert Trott and J. T. Hearne to score 44 and 83.

In September and October of that year Ranji took a side out to

America and Canada and naturally enough his great friends, MacLaren, Arthur Priestley and A. E. Stoddart, were the first to be invited. The full team was as follows:

K. S. Ranjitsinhji	B. J. T. Bosanquet
A. C. MacLaren	C. Robson
A. E. Stoddart	S. M. J. Woods
C. L. Townsend	G. C. B. Llewellyn
G. L. Jessop	W. P. Robertson
G. Brann	A. Priestley

'By long odds the greatest coterie of willow handlers that has ever invaded Uncle Sam's realm,' said *The American Cricketer* and indeed, with eight past or future Test players, it was a severe case of overkill. The local players, although they were overjoyed to be playing against such famous names – particularly Ranji who had so recently become first man to score 3,000 runs in a season – were a little disappointed in their own performances. Philadelphian society, however, was tremendously excited at the prospect of entertaining a real Prince and the most elaborate plans were laid for entertaining the team. Luckily for the 'fashionable set' the team 'were all college men and the social equals of the Prince', according to *The American Cricketer*.

The tourists played three games in Philadelphia, one against odds and two 'Tests' against the best of American cricket including the legendary J. B. King. Philadelphia were a strong team at this time, having beaten the 1896 Australians, but both 'Tests' were lost by an innings and over 100 runs, Archie putting on a dazzling display in the first. He scored 149 in just over three hours and King finished with one for 102. It was perhaps this innings that inspired an anecdote which was often repeated by Archie in later years. The local ground was girdled by trees beyond which was a ring of red-roofed houses, one boasting a single blue tile just below the chimney pot. When he went in to bat MacLaren inquired why this was, and was told that some years previously the Australian, Bonnor, had broken the slate with a six. 'That's nothing, I'll break

the next tile to it,' replied Archie. At this point in the tale some-
body could always be relied on to ask, 'And did you?' The ageing
Archie would rise to his full height, bang the floor with his walking-
stick and reply with perfect timing, 'My eye was completely out, I
missed by several tiles.'

MacLaren also scored 50 in the second 'Test' but was possibly
not so enthusiastic in the other games. The scorecard for one
match in New York contains the following curious entry:

| A. C. MacLaren | absconded | 0 |
| A. Priestley | absconded | 0 |

The pair had apparently stayed on to watch Sir Thomas Lipton's
yacht, *Shamrock*, challenge for the America's Cup. Archie's
absence was perhaps a little more surprising as he was supposedly
captain in this game with Ranji not playing.

At times the tourists found the cricket rather too easy, and
doubtless they occasionally gave the impression of being a little
superior. Archie was probably as guilty as anybody; indeed, during
the beer match that followed the early finish of the first 'Test' he at
times played the bowling with the handle of his bat. The local press
also complained that the fielding was listless and slapdash but the
tourists can hardly be blamed for treating the whole affair as a
holiday.

There were several amusing items in the American press at the
time, one introducing MacLaren as the man 'who was once three
entire days at the wicket, during which he piled up the enormous
total of 640 runs'. On the occasion when MacLaren did not bat
against New York a more serious note was struck: 'Tact and good
breeding are matters of refinement and are largely inborn, and it is,
perhaps, hardly fair to expect a display of these qualities among the
members of a team which was doubtless selected on account of the
cricketing prowess of its members rather than by reason of any very
intimate knowledge on their part of the often exacting usages of
polite society.' A sentence which could doubtless be applied to
many a cricket tour both before and since!

6
The Peak

The dawn of the twentieth century was to presage a new era for Archie who could now look forward for the first time to a full season as captain of Lancashire. At twenty-eight years of age he was at the height of his powers as a batsman and was the rightful captain of England, having behind him the experience of two Australian tours, three Test match centuries, a world record score and the tough baptism of 1899. The Lancashire team was becoming a formidable one, and although Albert Ward was still going strong, the first three in the batting order would soon read A. C. MacLaren, R. H. Spooner and J. T. Tyldesley. Perhaps just as important, a young boy named Neville Cardus was introduced to the wonders of Old Trafford and became enthralled with the heroes whose deeds inspired him to write about cricket in a style seldom approached before or since. The dazzling batting of the Lancashire side was one of the features of surely the greatest years in cricket's history.

Before the 1900 season began Archie's financial position took several turns for the better, enabling him to give up the teaching job which had kept him away from cricket in the past. The Lancashire club announced the appointment of MacLaren as assistant secretary, a post which he was to hold for the next three years. MacLaren did no administrative work, despite this title, and was regarded as being club coach; and since his coaching activities were confined solely to captaining the first XI, he was in fact being paid to play cricket. It has been reported that he received as much as £40 per week but unfortunately the Lancashire club records are incomplete for these years and the figure cannot be verified. He now earned enough to live on and during the summer his income was supplemented by reporting the Lancashire matches for the *Daily Express*. The copy had to be sent by seven o'clock in the evening which meant that occasionally there was only half an hour after leaving the field in which to write up the day's play. In these situations it was all hands to the pumps, contributions being made by the other players and even the pavilion attendant, Billy Howard. During this period it was common practice for the less well-to-do amateurs such as MacLaren, Fry and Jessop to contribute regularly to newspapers and magazines. Archie's output was large but he could never compete with C. B. Fry who in 1904 was, according to *The Bystander*, 'as usual, at the head of the cricket averages with the magnificent record of 168 columns and 5 magazine articles for the first month of the season. Mr MacLaren is a poor second, with 59 columns and a solitary magazine article.'

A sad event in March was the death in Guernsey of Archie's father, James, at the early age of 54. He had done so much for his sons and had been tremendously proud of them, especially Archie.

When the start of the new season arrived, MacLaren embarked on the job of leading his team like a general approaches a battle and his influence was immediately felt as they won all of the first seven matches. It may be that the thoroughness with which he was leading the campaign momentarily affected his batting but, after dropping himself down to number seven for one game, his form returned with a vengeance at Southampton. Having scored a rapid 79 in the first innings, Archie then chose to go for quick runs and a declaration in the second rather than enforce the follow on. In ten minutes on the second evening he made 17 not out and decided that an hour's batting next day should be enough. In fact it took him a further sixty-five minutes to reach his hundred at which point he declared. Most of his seventeen boundaries came from fierce blows between long-on and square leg.

During the following weeks he suffered a string of low scores, although the county were still unbeaten when they arrived at

Bristol. The old firm of MacLaren and Ward needed only one look at the wicket to know that this was their day, and at lunch the score was 156 for no wicket with Archie 103 not out. After two days of high scoring the only way Lancashire could gain the maximum points necessary for their championship hopes was to give Gloucestershire a target to chase on the last afternoon. MacLaren, though, in one of his recurrent moments of caprice, completely miscalculated and suffered some tremendous criticism in the press. At lunch Lancashire were 405 ahead with only three and a half hours left for play, but Archie was so obsessed with the perfect wicket and the ominous potential of Jessop in the opposition that he refused to declare. When the target had become completely impossible he eventually closed the innings and Gloucestershire were able to escape with a draw at 224 for nine. It was generally agreed that the Lancashire captain had received just what he deserved for an uncharacteristically defensive attitude, and the points lost were to be a subject of much regret by the end of the season.

The next match of the western tour, at Taunton, was won by an innings, with MacLaren for the second successive game powering to a century before lunch. A couple of weeks later Somerset (how he loved their bowling!) again suffered in the return at Old Trafford, the statistics this time being 108 in 105 minutes and a partnership of 159 with Albert Ward.

Archie's form about this time was irresistible, the next match with Sussex being launched by a gem of a MacLaren innings of 58 out of the first 67. At Worcester, though, he suffered a bad injury to his leg when Wilson, a fast bowler, hit him three times on the same spot, causing him to miss the following game, his only absence of the season. A quiet spell followed but he finished the season very much in the ascendancy with three very rapid fifties and finally a prodigious effort in the last game of the season against Leicestershire at Old Trafford. MacLaren wanted quick runs in the second innings to enable him to declare, but in the event he closed at 215 for four, last man 145! The innings progressed as follows:

> 50 in   35 minutes (MacLaren 42)
> 100 in   55 minutes (MacLaren 79)
> 215 in 115 minutes' (MacLaren 145).

His own century came up in only eighty minutes.

Despite the endless glut of runs, Lancashire yet again finished the season as runners up in the championship to an unbeaten Yorkshire. The summer had been one of unending success for Archie as both batsman and captain, except for the crucial error in the Gloucestershire game which still rankled with many. One critic commented, 'A lot of credit is due to Mr MacLaren for the manner in which he has handled the team. It seems to be the general impression that the professionals do not like him, but this is a great mistake . . . he has their utmost respect.' A cause for concern this season was the no-balling of Mold by Jim Phillips, an umpire who was leading a campaign to eliminate this doubtful action from the game. In December there was a meeting of the county captains during which MacLaren was the only representative to vote that Mold's action was fair. The Lancashire skipper outlined his views in a letter to the *Sportsman* newspaper, but Mold's illustrious career was about to come to an abrupt end.

The following season, 1901, was for many reasons not such a successful one for Archie. In his first twenty-five innings he had but one score over 50 and he missed several matches through illness and injury. His list of complaints read like a medical dictionary: to his old troubles of rheumatism and neuralgia were added a badly bruised thumb, a battered leg and even insomnia. He tried batting at six, seven, eight and even nine but to no effect. None of this helped Lancashire and even his captaincy suffered at times. As so often, though, it was a fellow player's benefit match which brought out his best. On this occasion it was in honour of the hero of Melbourne, J. T. Brown, that he knuckled down, played himself in and fought his way to 117 in the slow (by MacLaren standards) time of three and a half hours. The third hero of that famous Test match of six years earlier, Albert Ward, also scored a hundred. There can be no doubting Archie's determination in this match, and, despite his sequence of low scores he had encouraged the club treasurer, Jimmy Horner, to lay £10 on a MacLaren century. Another, more bizarre, detail concerning this innings is that it was played with an old bat which appeared to be made of polished mahogany. Archie had been given the bat, one of the presentation type never intended for actual play, by a boy at Harrow who received in exchange one of MacLaren's own bats. Nobody else would have contemplated using this curious weapon even at practice, but Archie was determined to prove that he had discovered something special. Years later the relic was smashed up, much to MacLaren's annoyance. Ranji, who knew nothing of the bat, was given it by Walter Brearley as a joke in the nets, and unfortunately it could no longer withstand the impact of a cricket ball.

For the rest of the season runs came with greater ease and he just managed to complete 1,000 runs, even though the old fluency was not always in evidence. In the last match, against Leicestershire, he took H. G. Garnett with him to open the innings with just over an hour left for play. At the close it was a familiar score, 112 for no wicket, but surprisingly the distribution was 25 to MacLaren and 82 to Garnett, who was enjoying an excellent season. Next morning, however, as if to show that he was still the master, Archie added 89 in eighty-five minutes. Even Johnny Tyldesley, who was in superlative form this season, was overshadowed, scoring 10 to Archie's 59.

It has been mentioned that MacLaren's captaincy did not escape criticism during this 1901 season. Against Derbyshire there was an eccentric declaration, and in addition he was well and truly slated after the match with Sussex. Winning the toss on a wet wicket, he asked the opposition to bat first and watched them casually run up 457 of which Ranji made 204 after being dropped with his score on 6. The most furious controversy of the year surrounded the Lancashire fast bowler, Arthur Mold, whose action had been condemned as unfair by the county captains in 1900. The matter came to a climax in the Somerset game when Jim Phillips no-balled Mold eighteen times for throwing. MacLaren, foreseeing a showdown, had asked A. N. Hornby before the match what course of action he would like to see should Phillips persistently call no-ball. The answer was that whatever happened Hornby would like to see Mold given a good bowl; this is why he was not simply taken off by MacLaren.

Another feature of the 1901 season at Old Trafford was the terrible state of the wicket which caused not only many injuries but also the dismissal of Lancashire by George Hirst for a paltry 44. During the winter an inadequately sieved dressing had apparently been applied to the square, resulting in small pebbles appearing on the wicket. Things came to a head when a ball from Kortright knocked out Johnny Tyldesley, and at the next committee meeting a furious MacLaren marched in and flung onto the table a handful of stones which he had collected from the pitch.

The 1901 season had been a busy one for Archie who spent much of his time organising a team to tour Australia under his leadership during the forthcoming winter. The tour was the last to be sent privately, the MCC being responsible for the financing and selection of English sides from 1903–4 onwards. Indeed, this idea had been mooted for some years and in August 1899 Major Wardill, the secretary of the Melbourne Cricket Club, had invited the MCC to send out a team in 1901–2. When the time came the MCC found that they could not raise a representative side and withdrew from the agreement. Since the Australian public had by now become convinced that the tour was a certainty, a telegram was hurriedly dispatched to MacLaren, who agreed to raise a team himself. In the event this task proved more difficult than he had imagined. Just as the MCC had discovered, the leading amateurs, Fry, Ranji, Jackson and R. E. Foster, were not available, nor were Hirst, Rhodes, Lockwood, Abel and Richardson among the professionals. Lord Hawke, the Yorkshire overlord, would not allow Hirst or Rhodes to tour, ostensibly because the Yorkshire club preferred them to rest during the winter, a decision which caused considerable friction between MacLaren and Hawke. His Lordship also maintained in an article in *Cricket* that there were financial considerations: 'I did not see why our players should go merely to put money into the hands of the Melbourne club. Only £300 each had been offered Rhodes and Hirst for the tour, whereas Richardson was paid £500. It was all a question of money, and a bigger offer might have had a different result.'

It was argued that the terms offered—£300 plus expenses and £25 beer money—were far more than the cricketers would earn normally in an English winter, but the fact that some of the professionals were paid more than others did cause ill-feeling. Incidentally, the amateurs were said to have received all their expenses plus a sum in three figures as pin-money. One of the side was even provided with the suit in which he embarked from England as an inducement to join the party.

Despite all this wrangling over payments many believed that the real reason for Hawke's intransigent attitude was a personal conflict with MacLaren. It had been reported that the abandoned MCC tour was to have included Hawke as manager/captain, with MacLaren as captain in the Tests. These plans were quite advanced, including arrangements to take sixteen players, when the project was cancelled because of the non-availability of the leading amateurs. The bitter pill for Hawke was that MacLaren himself was one of these 'unavailable' amateurs. According to Archie's own account he had been asked by Hawke soon after the invitation had been received from Melbourne whether he would join the party as captain, but he had begged time to consider owing to the illness of his father. Later MacLaren, hearing that there were difficulties over the tour, went to Lord's where W. G. Grace and A. E. Stoddart informed him of the non-availability of Jackson and company. Since he believed the project was now hopeless, he informed Hawke of his own withdrawal. One can well imagine Hawke's annoyance when he found MacLaren requesting the release of Hirst and Rhodes for his own private tour. The whole confusing business is perhaps best rationalised when one considers that MacLaren would have received only his expenses on an MCC tour, but was well rewarded for rescuing the Melbourne club with his own XI.

In the end MacLaren managed to gather a reasonable side, although the press were far from enthusiastic about their chances.

Many of the team have since become famous names but at the time three of the main bowlers had never appeared in a Test. Barnes, Blythe, Jessop and Braund were all relatively unknown quantities, and only MacLaren and Hayward had visited Australia before. The choice of Barnes was the most surprising. A league bowler, he had taken seven wickets in six games for Warwickshire and Lancashire between 1894 and 1899, before re-appearing in Lancashire's last fixture of 1901 against Leicestershire at Old Trafford. In this one match he took six for 70 and so impressed MacLaren that he was immediately offered a county contract for 1902 and an invitation to tour Australia. The ultimate success of this decision was a marvellous tribute to Archie's speed and accuracy in assessing a player's ability. The fact that he backed this judgement by actually picking the unknown Barnes for England was also typical of MacLaren. The public were amazed. 'Who is Barnes?' queried one newspaper, while another suggested MacLaren was a suitable candidate for the lunatic asylum. Archie, as always, was impervious to such criticism. This was the first time he had ever had full selectoral control and, considering his difficulties, he met with tremendous success. Not only was the selection of Barnes a masterstroke, but that of Blythe and Braund was almost as prophetic. Characteristically, MacLaren showed unshakeable confidence in his own selections and publicly defended his team at every opportunity.

Detailed accounts of the trip are hard to come by, perhaps because no tour book was written. Ranji had penned a comprehensive journal of Stoddart's last venture and from 1903–4 onwards there are a succession of full descriptions from authors such as Warner, Hobbs and Fender. For MacLaren's side there is no such permanent record and even the full scores of some of the matches are impossible to obtain. This is surprising since at the time there was considerable public interest in the matches. We are also robbed of the type of detail that is seldom found in newspaper reports, such as a comparison between the two captains, MacLaren and Darling. There were many good performances, notably from MacLaren himself, but the brilliant young Australian team had reached its peak and England were defeated in the series by four matches to one as in 1897–8. Perhaps the writing was on the wall from the very first match against South Australia, which began only five days after the team's arrival aboard the s.s. *Omrah*. Not even the full quota of shipboard exercise ordered by MacLaren was enough to offset this disadvantage. Notwithstanding excellent perform- ances with the ball by Barnes (four for 32) and Blythe (five for 45), the English XI were overwhelmed by 233 runs. The tourists had the first of many sights of Clem Hill (107 and 80) and even suffered at the hands of the veteran George Giffen who had long since retired from the Test match scene.

The team's next stop was Victoria where, much to Archie's annoyance, they were too late for the Melbourne Cup. In his speech at the local Town Hall, MacLaren managed to include the state- ment that he wished there were a few more sportsmen on the York- shire county committee at the present time, an obvious allusion to Lord Hawke. It was not long either, before Archie crossed swords with the local cricket administrators in the shape of the New South Wales Cricket Association, the same body who had withdrawn their wedding gift four years previously after another MacLaren disagreement. This time the reason was the appointment of umpires for the tour matches. Formerly it had been standard prac- tice for the visitors to be allowed to nominate one umpire for each game but NSW wanted the practice discontinued. Archie made his point with typical bluntness in a telegram which read, 'The right of appointing one umpire is mine entirely and must request your association allow me to make appointment.' The general feeling outside New South Wales was in favour of MacLaren who also promised the support of four county captains for a reciprocal agree- ment in England. This inducement finally did the trick and the choice of one umpire remained with MacLaren.

The match in Melbourne produced a good win thanks mainly to Barnes who took twelve for 99, but MacLaren was prevented from playing by an attack of rheumatism. Fortunately this cleared up in time for him to renew his acquaintance with the Sydney Cricket Ground. This he did in no uncertain fashion, scoring 145 and 73 in two flawless displays. Never has the art of batsmanship been consummated more fully than when MacLaren reigned at Sydney. The local spectators warmed to him as enthusiastically as did those of Manchester or Liverpool, and on this occasion his reception was rapturous. Len Braund also performed heroically for the first of many times on the tour to take twelve wickets for 239 runs, but the match was narrowly lost. The New South Wales second innings recovered from 115 for seven to 399 for eight while MacLaren's misgivings about the Australian umpires were apparently substantiated. Johnny Tyldesley in a letter to England wrote, 'We ought to have won the NSW game, but the umpire made a lot of blunders, and the decision when he gave Mr Jones out was cruel – even the bowler said so.'

This game with New South Wales was followed by only two more first-class fixtures between the first and fifth Tests, practice being confined to minor, country games against odds. Although the English XI were generally overwhelmingly successful against these teams, their first meeting with one must have been a salutary experience. Entering the game against Northern Districts at West Maitland with a weak bowling side, MacLaren's men fielded out while the local XVII amassed 558 for fifteen before having the cheek to declare.

Nevertheless, the tourists arrived at Sydney for the opening Test match in confident mood. MacLaren doubtless remembered that on both of Stoddart's tours England had started the series with a win on this very ground. All that was needed was for Archie to win the toss and score his almost inevitable century, and the sequence would surely be extended. This scenario could scarcely have been followed more accurately.

MacLaren's first decision, after electing to take first innings, was to open the batting with himself and Surrey's Tom Hayward. In the last Test of 1899 he had promoted Hayward to open, with inspiring results. Now Archie's encyclopaedic cricketing brain recalled the day four years previously when, on this very ground, the Australian bowlers had toiled away at the broad bats of MacLaren and Hayward on a concrete-hard wicket. The decision may seem an obvious one with hindsight, but until MacLaren earmarked the Surrey stalwart as the ideal opener, Hayward had invariably batted in the middle of the order for both county and country. On this occasion the partnership prospered to the tune of 85 by lunch. Both batsmen leaned on all their experience, allowing the runs to accumulate steadily with the minimum of risk. MacLaren had not batted like this since the last tour to Australia. The reason why he always scored quicker and with more gusto in England was that he was never certain when the vagaries of the pitch would cut short his innings. In Australia both he and Hayward knew that runs would come in perfect safety.

Shortly before lunch Archie experienced a bad patch, remaining on 46 for some time before being dropped in the slips off Ernest Jones. This escape proved vital, for during the afternoon session he moved remorselessly on, despite losing Hayward at 154. The varied attacks of Jones, Noble, McLeod, Howell, Trumble and Laver were reduced to impotence. Just as in his two centuries during the 1897–8 series, this was the responsible MacLaren determined to put his side in a winning position. As at lunch, he remained scoreless for several overs before the tea interval, resolved not to give away this hard-fought advantage. Immediately afterwards, however, he moved to his hundred with his seventeenth boundary, an off-drive against Laver, having batted eight minutes over three hours. This was one of five successive boundaries that took his score from 88 to 108. Now was the time to push the score on but, exhausted by his efforts, MacLaren soon missed a full pitch from McLeod which he tried to turn to leg and was dismissed lbw for 116. This was the fourth time he had scored a century in a Test, the first player ever to exceed three. It was also the last Test century by an England captain in Australia until Peter May scored 113 at Melbourne in 1958–9.

A minor collapse followed MacLaren's dismissal, but next day Lilley and Braund added a record 124 for the seventh wicket and the tail carried the score to 464. At last the moment had arrived. MacLaren's secret weapon, Sydney Francis Barnes, could be unleashed on the Australians. Barnes took the new ball and with only his second delivery in international cricket he caught and bowled the great Vic Trumper for just two runs. MacLaren's delight can be imagined, although his heart missed a beat as Barnes casually took the straightforward catch one-handed. During this second evening and on the following morning MacLaren kept Barnes bowling, virtually without a rest, until the innings was finished for a miserable 168. Barnes' analysis was five for 65 in 35.1 overs, the only disappointed person being the bowler himself, who thought the figures rather poor compared with his usual performances for Burnley. MacLaren's judgement had been vindicated for all the world to see.

Following on with the wicket still full of runs, Australia were bowled out again by the end of the third day to lose by an innings and 124 runs. This time they succumbed to the spin of Blythe and Braund who, with Barnes, took all twenty Australian wickets in the match. Each of these three was playing in his first Test match and each was a personal choice of MacLaren. We know that Barnes' selection caused astonishment but Ranji had also been quoted as saying that Blythe would not even get a single wicket on Australian soil. The match was a great personal triumph for Archie and the family scrapbook is full of the many congratulatory telegrams that poured in from all over the world. The cricketing public began to think again about England's 'second XI'.

Two country games followed before the second Test in Melbourne. In one of these the English team had to call on S. V. Green (a cousin of C. E. Green of Cambridge University, Essex, Middlesex and Sussex) to make up the XI, and in two later games S. M. J. Woods also assisted. Woods, who had played in Tests for both England and Australia, was in Australia visiting relatives and would have played in one of the Tests but for a too-hot Turkish bath the day before the game.

Australia brought in R. A. Duff and W. W. Armstrong for the second game and at last their great team was complete. The strongest of oppositions would have struggled against their talented combination but MacLaren's 'second XI' never gave up despite losing all of the remaining four Tests. The winning margins were 229 runs, four wickets, seven wickets and 32 runs, which was not a disgrace in the circumstances. The Melbourne game started well for England, Australia being dismissed for 112 after Archie had put them in on a wet wicket. Barnes showed that his Sydney performance was no fluke by taking six for 42 including Trumper, again with the second ball of the match. Blythe, with a badly split spinning finger, shared the wickets and the pair bowled unchanged, but some critics felt that one good change bowler might well have restricted the score to under a hundred. This lack of depth in bowling was to be exposed several times on the tour.

When England went in to bat with the wicket deteriorating minute by minute, MacLaren issued orders to get quick runs or get out, in order to make Australia bat again that day. Although Jessop scored 27 in twenty-one minutes, the rest failed badly against Noble (seven for 17) and were dismissed in just over an hour for 61. At the end of an eventful first day England had Australia struggling at 48 for five, all five wickets to Barnes. Darling, however, had outmanoeuvred Archie by changing his batting order and sacrificing his tail-enders while the wicket was at its worst. The next day the batting order from numbers six to eleven was Gregory, Hill, Trumper, Noble, Duff and Armstrong. Perhaps even more crucially, they had a vastly improved wicket to bat on, thanks to the groundsman who had dried the pitch overnight with blankets and rolling, contrary to the rules of the game. Australia eventually scored 353 with Duff and Armstrong, the two debutants, adding 120 for the last wicket. Duff top-scored in both innings with 32 and 104. For England, Barnes was tragically over-bowled, sending down forty-two consecutive overs before finishing with seven for 121 from sixty-four overs. MacLaren was criticised retrospectively for his merciless use of Barnes, but with the meagre bowling resources available he had little choice. F. A. Iredale, the old Australian player, noted prophetically in the *Daily Mail*, 'The match has shown the immense responsibility resting on Barnes. The magnitude of the work devolving upon him is enormous, and any accident to him would have enormous consequences for the team as a whole.'

Wanting 405 to win, England succumbed in their second innings to Noble and Trumble, the latter finishing the match with a hat-trick. MacLaren presented Barnes with the ball, suitably mounted, in recognition of his marvellous bowling. England had been soundly beaten and full credit must go to Joe Darling for his imaginative changes in the batting order, in conjunction of course with the unscheduled improvement in the wicket. With this defeat went any hopes of saving the series for, despite some heroic performances and a first innings lead in each of the three remaining matches, England's meagre bowling resources just could not follow up any breakthrough.

The next Test, at Adelaide, was the real turning point of the series and provided yet another example of the undisputed bad luck which the fates reserved for MacLaren. The England team were saddened by news of poor Johnny Briggs' death in England, but for the first day and a half everything went right, Braund (103 not out) and Quaife building on another masterful opening stand of 149 by Hayward and MacLaren. But when Australia batted disaster struck: Barnes had to leave the field. He was apparently wearing new spikes in his boots, which caused him to twist his knee so badly that he took no further part in the tour. England's attack, already severely stretched, was therefore deprived of its only match-winning spearhead. This disaster turned the whole series upside down for Barnes, who had taken nineteen wickets in four innings, would surely have ensured victory in this match and possibly even in the entire series.

In addition to this loss Colin Blythe was ordered by the doctor to rest his split finger. This left Len Braund and John Gunn to wheel away for hour after hour in the exhausting heat, their courageous effort on the third day giving England a lead of 67 which MacLaren and Hayward increased by 80 before a second innings wicket fell. Then Hugh Trumble gradually chipped away at the rest of the batting order until, after a delay caused by a dust storm, Australia were eventually left 315 to win. This far from easy task would surely have been beyond them if Barnes had been fit to bowl, but Clement Hill added 97 to his two previous innings of 99 and 98, and Darling and Trumble saw the home team to victory by four wickets. Even without Barnes, England might have won if Lilley had accepted a stumping chance from Hill when his score was only 19.

This great disappointment was followed by one of the highlights of the tour, and naturally enough the setting was the Sydney Cricket Ground. The return game with New South Wales started on a controversial note with MacLaren objecting to the appointed umpire, Crockett. The team had felt aggrieved at some of his past decisions and doubtless Archie found this the ideal opportunity to exercise the right which New South Wales had sought to deny him. He therefore nominated Charles Bannerman as substitute umpire amid considerable public debate. Archie was always quick to win a point once he 'had his fighting armour on', as he used to put it, and this time he did so by remembering that Darling had once asked the MCC not to appoint Mordecai Sherwin as an umpire in England.

Eventually the match could begin and the home team took first knock, scoring an impressive 432. This figure was soon dwarfed, however, as MacLaren's XI assembled the record total by an English team in Australia—769. The scorecard read:

A. C. MacLaren	167
T. W. Hayward	174
J. T. Tyldesley	142
W. G. Quaife	62
G. L. Jessop	87

Again it was the old firm of MacLaren and Hayward who set the innings off on the right foot with a magnificent partnership of 314 in under four hours. Archie reached his hundred after two hours ten minutes, Hayward's taking three hours. By the time MacLaren was dismissed the pair had broken the record for any wicket partnership in Australia. Johnny Tyldesley and Gilbert Jessop (87 in fifty-seven minutes) continued to plunder the bowling and with the score at 649 for three a new world record seemed certain, but overnight rain ruined the attempt. New South Wales were easily dismissed a second time to give the tourists an inspiring innings victory immediately before the next Test on the Sydney ground.

As in the two recent defeats England started promisingly but suffered defeat through lack of depth in bowling, Barnes having failed a fitness test on the morning of the match. MacLaren won the toss for the fourth successive time—nothing wrong with his luck here—and the now famous partnership of Hayward and his captain, followed by Johnny Tyldesley, took the score to 179 for one. At this point the left-handed Saunders, playing in his first Test, induced a collapse which left the final total at a rather disappointing 317, MacLaren top-scoring with 92. Gilbert Jessop then struck form for one of the few occasions throughout the tour, whistling out the first four Australians for only 48 thanks to some marvellous slip catches. Whatever their shortcomings MacLaren's team were the finest fielding side ever seen in Australia and the slip cordon of MacLaren, Braund and Jones was by all accounts breathtaking. Whenever Archie was responsible for the selection of a team he paid the greatest attention to fielding. Examples can be found in his faith in Jessop and his imaginative selections for the famous Eastbourne match of 1921. He reasoned, quite correctly, that if a fielder caught or ran out Trumper from a half chance, then any other contributions he might make were a bonus.

When Jessop's electric burst of speed was exhausted the Australians slowly began to accumulate runs against the slow spin of Braund and Blythe. The absence of Barnes was really felt now especially since his replacement, C. P. McGahey, was purely a batsman. As on the two previous tours by Stoddart, no bowling reserves were carried. Imagine what might have happened to those teams if, say, Tom Richardson had broken down. Batting a second time the England team inexplicably collapsed against Noble and Saunders for a pitiful 99, leaving Australia the victors by seven wickets.

Before the final Test, Archie ran up a quick century in a low scoring win against Victoria. With the series already decided England really should have won the fifth match in Melbourne but, through no fault of the perennially unlucky MacLaren, Australia scraped home by 32 runs. There were perhaps two decisive moments which contributed most to England's defeat. The first was in Australia's second innings when Lilley again dropped Hill, the batsman going on to score 87, the only half-century in the match. Then, with only 211 needed for victory in England's final innings, Archie took command and had imperiously stroked 49 out of 87 for two when Jessop ran him out in the last over of the second day's play. This effectively ended any hopes of a consolation win. MacLaren's form with the bat was still the highlight of the series and in the first innings, with quick runs the order of the day, he had opened with Jessop as his partner. The huge crowd at Melbourne were in luck for they witnessed a breathtaking partnership of 50 in just twenty minutes as Noble and Trumble were battered to all corners. Jessop and MacLaren in full flight together must have been an awesome sight.

The series had been a great frustration for MacLaren, knowing that he had come very close to an amazing victory yet in fact had lost 4−1. In addition to Barnes' incalculable loss, Lilley had experienced trouble with his hands throughout the tour, doubtless explaining the chances which he missed and which marred an otherwise exemplary fielding side. Percy Cross Standing, in his magazine *Cricket of Today and Yesterday*, concluded that, 'all things considered and weighed in the balance, Mr MacLaren's heavily-handicapped eleven have acquitted themselves exceedingly well while their commander's personal reputation alike as cricketer and captain has been immeasurably enhanced'. Indeed, MacLaren finished top of the national batting averages for the Australian season.

Archie's supposed pessimism was apparently never in evidence despite the defeats: 'Mr MacLaren was never depressed when things were going against us, and was always solicitous for the welfare of his team,' wrote A. A. Lilley.

Throughout the tour the English public were kept guessing by a succession of rumours regarding the possibility of MacLaren leaving the Lancashire club. Immediately before setting off for Australia he had sent a telegram to the club resigning both the captaincy and the post of assistant secretary. The following letter explained his reasons:

Eastrop House
Basingstoke,
24th Sept. 1901

Dear Mr Swire,

It is with the greatest reluctance that a combination of circumstances causes me to resign not only the assistant secretaryship of the club but also my connection with Lancashire cricket. My wife's health is such that it is no longer possible for me to leave her for any length of time. She is very delicate, and her doctor has advised me not to leave her. She is only just able to get about after her long illness. Which I hear will leave its mark. For these private reasons, and no other, do I feel bound to relinquish my position with Lancashire cricket. Last season the worry and anxiety of illness at home quite prevented me at times from concentrating my whole thoughts on the game. The kindness received at your hands, and others of the committee, will always be treasured by me, no captain ever getting better treatment than I did. Happiness of home comes before my county, and as it is my wife's wish for me to be near her I have decided to take this step, and am notifying the Hampshire committee to the effect that I will play for them next season.

Yours Sincerely,
A. C. MacLaren

The MacLarens now lived in Hampshire and although Maud's illness was not serious enough to stop her accompanying Archie to Australia, playing for Lancashire would certainly have kept him away from home. The news caused a great deal of conjecture at the time, especially the possibility of MacLaren playing for Hampshire. During the tour rumour and counter-rumour emerged from Australia including a report that Archie would settle in his wife's country of origin. Then the following quote appeared in the *South Australia Register*: 'It has been stated in the papers that the Hampshire club has offered me the post of assistant secretary with salary. As soon as I knew that this was correct, owing to receiving the full report of the meeting, I wrote home declining the post. It is, perhaps, unnecessary to add that I receive no salary from the club whatever.' MacLaren appears to have been most sensitive on the point of salary. At this time there was extensive gossip about certain amateurs receiving illicit payments, and the establishment felt so strongly on the subject that it eventually cost MacLaren the England captaincy.

On returning from Australia, Archie, finding that Lancashire had appointed Alec Eccles as captain, stated that he would continue to live in Hampshire but was unsure for whom he would play. In April the matter was clarified when MacLaren announced that his wife's health had recovered sufficiently in Australia for him to continue playing for Lancashire as a 'freelance'. In May this decision was confirmed by the Lancashire committee and Archie was reappointed as captain for 1902; Eccles sportingly stood down and continued to appear occasionally for Lancashire until 1907.

An amusing sidelight to this saga was provided by *Punch* which lampooned MacLaren by awarding him the world record for the longest sentence, to match his record 424. In a letter to the Lancashire club he wrote, 'Having returned from Australia feeling stronger than I have done for years, having practically banished all rheumatism, owing to a cure that I have been undergoing for the last four months, coupled with the fact that Mrs MacLaren has also benefited, I am perfectly willing still to do my best to play for Lancashire, always provided the Lancashire people wish to see me again, although it is quite impossible for me to accept the post which has been offered to me, which is considerably more remunerative than the last one, owing to the necessity of my being free to return home at any time when my presence is required there.'

7
Vintage Summer – 1902

Most cricket historians will agree that for exciting finishes, out-standing individual performances and endless talking points, the 1902 Test series has never been surpassed. The real reason why these matches come alive, even for those who never saw them, is the quality of the players concerned. Just to recount their names encapsulates all that the Golden Age meant, and who today would not dream of being transported to the summer of 1902, even if it did rain more than usual? Trumper, Duff, Hill, Darling, Noble, Gregory, Armstrong, MacLaren, Palairet, Tyldesley, Jackson, Hayward, Jessop, Ranji and Fry: any two of these would make a match memorable but this list contains fifteen names, all in their prime and all attractive strokemakers.

Close inspection of the two teams fails to reveal a single chink in their armour. This equality of the sides had its natural consequence in the famous cliff-hanger finishes described so vividly on many occasions, especially by Sir Neville Cardus and Richard Binns. Still, as in any game, one team had to lose and in this case it was England. Although the reasons for this have been discussed over and over again, with indifferent team selection and captaincy the leading candidates for blame, they bear re-scrutiny. Since assuming the England captaincy MacLaren had succeeded in winning only two out of twelve games, although his captaincy as such had never been seriously faulted. Now, for the first time, the spotlight fell on his every move, the more so because the games were so close.

Before the first Test Archie was in excellent form for Lancashire and it was more than once remarked how much more alert and lithe he looked after his winter in the warmth of Australia. His batting as well as his health appear to have returned to the status of two years earlier. 'Last year his lack of restraint and his desire to get most of his runs by leg strokes and hooks often caused him to sacrifice his wicket in a ruthless manner so that the change in his method at the outset proves how he has benefited from Australia and that MacLaren is himself again.' This newspaper comment followed his first innings of the season which, like his last innings of the previous summer, was a century against Leicestershire.

It was at this time that Lancashire followed the example of Yorkshire and abolished the custom whereby amateurs and professionals took the field from different pavilion gates. This decision owed much to MacLaren's initiative and further gave the lie to the belief that he was aloof from the professionals. Nothing gave him greater pleasure than the tremendous cheers when he walked down the pavilion steps for the first time alongside Albert Ward to open against Sussex.

Birmingham was the venue for the first of the five battles with Australia. Archie was raring to go and had been planning the campaign meticulously by sending and receiving reports on the current form of both sets of players. On the day before the Test he was in such a hurry that he knocked off the 89 needed to beat Gloucestershire in only thirty-five minutes, his own contribution being 56 not out.

The England team for this first Test can hardly be faulted and it is often referred to as England's greatest ever XI, although Sydney Barnes might have a few words to say about that. MacLaren won the toss and batted first on a good but slow wicket under ominous dark clouds. C. B. Fry fell to the lightning pace of Ernest Jones for nought and MacLaren was badly run out by Ranji for 9. The latter received considerable castigation in the press, one cartoon representing MacLaren as a headmaster chastising Ranji the schoolboy dunce. England recovered, however, thanks to Johnny Tyldesley with help from Jackson and Hirst, and carried the score to 351 for nine at the close of an eventful day. Overnight there was rain, heavy enough to prevent a resumption until 3.10 the next after-noon by which time the wicket had deteriorated, the light was poor and the atmosphere highly charged. After half an hour MacLaren declared in order to expose the Australians to the drying pitch and Hirst and Rhodes opened the bowling to the dangerous Trumper and Duff. At first the pair survived, but MacLaren astutely gave Braund a solitary over to change the bowlers' ends and the rest of the innings became a procession. The might of the Australian XI fell in only one and a half hours for a trifling 36 runs. Unfortunately further heavy rain left the game tantalisingly drawn on the last day, even though the players went through the motions for just over an hour purely to satisfy the 10,000 spectators who had queued for admission.

In this worst of English summers, rain followed the two teams to Headingley where the second game was abandoned with England 102 for two and MacLaren 47 not out. After this Archie hardly scored a run for Lancashire, and he offered to stand down from the third Test at Sheffield, an idea that was of course squashed by the selectors. His form returned just before the Test with an inn-ings of 174 against Nottinghamshire during the course of which he added a hundred before lunch on the second day. Again it was noticed in the Press how his attitude to batting, which had become rather careless, had improved: 'Mr MacLaren has altogether aban-doned that half reckless fashion of trying to knock the bowling about from the very start.'

It was during this match at Trent Bridge that Ranji cabled MacLaren as follows, 'Much regret inability to play tomorrow. Snapped calf muscle. Hoped against hope to be fit. Cannot field or put pressure on leg.' Ranji's withdrawal gained a last minute reprieve for the out-of-form C. B. Fry and Schofield Haigh was added to the XI, the final place resting between him and Lockwood. Although the English were confident, the Australians had sur-vived a host of injuries and illness without losing either of the Tests and they could now include their best bowler, Hughie Trumble.

At nine o'clock on the morning of the match Sydney Barnes,

sitting at home in Manchester, received an urgent message from MacLaren to the effect that he was to play at Sheffield that morning. Barnes' knee injury of the previous winter had been cured shortly after his return but he had not shown peak fitness or form in the early part of the season. In the last two Lancashire games, however, he had bowled particularly well and MacLaren greeted Lord Hawke at Sheffield with the suggestion that he should play to the exclusion of both Haigh and Lockwood, an idea that his Lordship supported.

Barnes duly arrived at the ground with the match already under way, just in time to see Trumper clean bowled by Braund for only one.

At this stage Clem Hill, Australia's number three, emerged from the pavilion followed by Barnes. The subsequent departure of the twelfth man, Haigh, produced a spate of booing and jeering from the chauvinistic Yorkshire crowd who had assumed that their local hero was playing. One bystander was heard to taunt Lord Hawke with, 'Here is one of the unfortunate selectors, and he a Yorkshireman!' A member of the press box even typed out the message, 'Lancashire's lame duckling was preferred to Haigh.' This type of reception had a galvanising effect on the quixotic Barnes and before long MacLaren introduced him in place of the successful Braund, another move which was unpopular with the locals. Barnes made his point immediately, having Hill caught by Rhodes with his second ball and Darling taken in the slips immediately afterwards for nought. The Australians could only partially recover from these setbacks to muster 194, Barnes taking six for 49 to bring his tally in only two and a half games against the old enemy to twenty-five wickets.

After tea MacLaren and Abel, the diminutive 'Guv'nor' and darling of the Oval crowd, cruised to 61 at a run a minute before Noble slowed the rate by bowling both openers. The light was by now very poor as F. S. Jackson and Johnny Tyldesley nudged the score to 101 for two at six o'clock. An appeal against the conditions would almost certainly have been upheld but the decision was delayed a crucial fifteen minutes by which time the score had become a disastrous 102 for five. It was at this point that the umpires eventually suspended play for the day. MacLaren must take a share of the blame for this failure to lodge an appeal but it was also generally agreed that an error had been made in holding a Test match on the notoriously murky Sheffield ground. Jessop had some harsh words to say on this subject and C. B. Fry claimed that he never saw the ball from which he was stumped.

Next day England were dismissed 49 in arrears and then the old MacLaren injury jinx struck again. This time Barnes' knee injury did not cause his complete withdrawal, but it did render him totally ineffective. Vic Trumper launched the Australian second innings with 62 in only fifty minutes, and Clem Hill effectively won the match and the series with 119 in two and a half hours. Requiring 339 to win, a daunting task, England had ninety minutes to bat on the second evening in poor light and with rain threatening. It was time for another MacLaren inspiration. Who else would have sent Gilbert Jessop out to open the innings at such a time? He must surely be mad, thought the spectators, as they began to reach for raincoats and umbrellas.

At 14 the nervous Bobby Abel was caught in the slips, a decision he hotly disputed, but after only an hour's play the score was 73 for one. The incredible Jessop was 53 not out, but at this point he was dropped in the deep causing the umpires to judge the light too bad for play, having refused an appeal fifteen minutes earlier. The question on everybody's lips was, 'Can England and Jessop do the impossible?' Perhaps another thirty minutes of good light that evening would have seen the 'Croucher's' own century and England on the road to victory, but it was not to be. On the last day Noble and Trumble swept aside the rest of the batting including Jessop, lbw to a full toss which hit him on the chest! Only MacLaren provided any resistance with a real captain's innings of 63, his half-century taking forty minutes including an onslaught of 21 in five balls. Alas, nobody could stay with him and the match was lost by 143 runs, a convincing margin, but the story could have been so different had Barnes remained fit and if play had been suspended earlier on that vital first evening.

This Sheffield victory gave the Australians all the confidence they needed to forget the early season misfortunes and move on to the Old Trafford match firing on all cylinders. This fourth Test is surely as famous as any in the history of the game—Tate's match. Historians have usually blamed poor Fred Tate for dropping a catch and not scoring those last 4 runs and thereby losing a series which England should have won. In fact the series was really lost at Sheffield since the nail-biting encounters in the final two Tests really balance each other out. Seldom is enough credit given for the victory which was won by surely one of the strongest combinations ever to represent Australia.

The selectors, Hawke, MacGregor and Bainbridge, plus Jackson and Steel who were co-opted, had plenty to consider after Sheffield and quite rightly brought Ranji back in place of Fry. To universal amazement, however, Jessop was dropped in favour of the Somerset opener, Lionel Palairet. Surely there should have been room for the 'Croucher', who had just scored that dazzling fifty at Sheffield and was worth a place for his fielding alone? Archie's absence and F. S. Jackson's presence on the selection committee may well have been the reason, for while MacLaren was a fervent pro-Jessopian the more conservative Yorkshireman always considered the Gloucestershire man rather a gamble.

Quite rightly Lockwood was restored to the side in the absence of the ailing Barnes, and if this had been the full extent of the selectors' decisions (as it was in the first press announcement) no doubt the omission of Jessop could have been forgiven. It transpired, though, that the meeting of the committee had been further complicated by the decision to add a wet-wicket specialist to the XI, an insurance should the weather prove inclement on the day of the game. At the time there was only one man in England for such a job, Schofield Haigh of Yorkshire. It was now that the vested interests and egoism of Lord Hawke took a hand, initiating the chain of events which culminated in defeat at Old Trafford. Since the weather was sunny and apparently set fair for some time, Lord Hawke was disinclined to see Schofield Haigh kicking his heels as twelfth man in Manchester when he could be playing for a Yorkshire team who would already be without Rhodes, Hirst and

Jackson. For this reason the autocratic chairman over-ruled his co-selectors and insisted that Fred Tate of Sussex would be adequate as the extra bowler since he was unlikely to be needed anyway. Tate was in excellent form and was to take 180 wickets that season, but the way in which Lord Hawke again allowed the interests of Yorkshire to dictate to England made MacLaren livid when he heard of it. It was often said that Hawke had lost more Test matches against Australia than anyone else although he had never played in one. It was the inclusion of Tate and the omission of Jessop that prompted the famous MacLaren quote, 'My God, look what they've given me! Do they think we are playing the blind asylum?' since reported in various forms by Cardus and Jimmy Catton amongst others.

The morning of the first day, like so many others during Manchester Tests, dawned wet and miserable. MacLaren arrived at the ground still furious at Hawke's high-handed attitude and, no doubt, remembering the previous occasions when he had been on the receiving end of his Lordship's obsession with his adopted county (Lord Hawke was born in Lincolnshire). Being MacLaren, there was only one way he could re-act—the wicket was wet, Tate had been chosen as wet-wicket bowler, therefore Tate would play. Who was he to leave out? Two could play at Lord Hawke's game; Hirst, another Yorkshireman and hero of the first Test, would stand down and act as twelfth man. This superb irony doubtless delighted MacLaren and infuriated Hawke.

It seems incredible to see the chairman of the selectors putting personal motives before his country and the England captain, in a fit of pique, putting revenge before the winning of a Test. Not that the public were aware of this in-fighting: in fact one newspaper said of Tate, 'Succeed or not, he was on general form the man for the wicket which we may yet have.'

The heavy rain resulted in the wicket starting dead on the first morning but it would gradually become more spiteful as the sun set to work. Australia won the toss and the subtlety of the situation was not lost on either of those two master tacticians, Darling and MacLaren. Australia's need was for quick runs before the wicket became sticky, and MacLaren's to perform a holding operation until that time. But his carefully laid plans to that end were swept aside by the opening pair, Trumper and Duff, who put on 135 in only ninety minutes, the score being 173 for one at lunch. The story of how 'the subtlest of England's cricket captains concentrated all his craft in reducing Trumper to immobility' has been beautifully captured by Cardus. 'Once at a dinner when it was suggested to Archie that he had slipped up, MacLaren, who adored an argument, rose to the bait; he took lumps of sugar out of the basin and set them all over the table, saying ''Gaps be damned! Good God, I knew my man—Victor had half a dozen strokes for the same kind of ball. I exploited the inner and outer ring—a man there, a man there, and another man covering him.'' (He banged the lumps of sugar down one by one, punctuating his luminous discourse.) ''I told my bowlers to pitch on the short side to the off: I set my heart and brain on every detail of our policy. Well, in the third over of the morning Victor hit two balls straight into the practice ground, high over the screen, behind the bowler. I couldn't very well have had a man fielding in the bloody practice ground, now could I?'' '

After lunch the wicket was at its worst and Australia collapsed against Lockwood and Rhodes. England, in turn, were only saved from ignominy by Jackson and Braund who managed to hang on and reach 70 for five by the close of an eventful first day. Next morning the weather had cleared and Jackson (128) and Braund (65) were solely responsible for the England score approaching within 37 of Australia. With two and a half hours left for play Trumper and Duff opened again but there was to be no repeat of that first day as an inspired Lockwood shot out this pair and Hill with the score only 10. The new batsman, Skipper Darling, immediately skied Braund to deep square leg where Fred Tate dropped the chance. The importance of this cannot be overestimated as Darling eventually scored 37 out of a paltry total of 86. Since that day there has been much ill-informed comment to the effect that Tate should never have been stationed on the boundary as he always fielded in the slips for Sussex. When this theory was repeated in *The Times* during the summer of 1919,

MacLaren was moved to reply in full to that newspaper. His long letter is reproduced here, perhaps for the first time; it provides the most detailed account of how the presence of a left-handed and a right-handed batsman caused the Tate incident.

Dear Sir,

I forward facts which can be corroborated by such as Braund, the bowler, or Lilley, the wicket-keeper, who heard the conversations which took place.

When Darling faced Braund after a single by Gregory, the point and mid-off to him were then the only two men on the on-side. With Darling facing Braund these naturally should fall back on the leg boundary for the left-handed batsman as no less than five of the seven fieldsmen on the leg side to Gregory had to cross over to the leg side for Darling after a single had been scored. L. C. H. Palairet was moved the whole length of the ground, from the leg boundary when Gregory received the ball, to the leg boundary behind the umpire when Darling faced Braund. The Maharaja Ranjitsinjhi was dead lame, and consequently was useless as an out-fielder, since he would have made little or no ground to a catch, and for that reason I refused his offer to fall back. As Darling was hitting out at every ball I felt that, with the great amount of what became off-break to the left-handed batsman, Braund was getting on the ball, the spin would most likely cause Darling's hit to carry behind rather than in front of the square leg boundary, and I accordingly placed Lionel Palairet in that position with Tate in front. Braund then asked me if he might not have L. C. H. Palairet in front where Tate was fielding, and although I pointed out that the finer long-leg was more likely to get the catch, he still preferred to have Lionel Palairet in front where Tate was fielding, and as I never went against any bowler of judgement, Tate was allowed to take the fine-leg position and Palairet came in front to occupy the position in which he usually fielded for Somerset. Tate got the catch and had the misfortune to drop it. No one was more sorry for Tate than myself and, although I had the greatest respect for Tate as a bowler, it was in my opinion far too late in his career to ask him to play for his first time at so critical a period in the Test games. When we were one down with only two games to play. Your correspondent says that he cannot vouch for it, but the story goes that both the Hon. F. S. Jackson and Ranjitsinjhi offered to take the long field. The Hon. F. S. Jackson, a fine in-field, on the contrary asked to be allowed to retain that position.

Your correspondent says that short slip and mid-on were the only two places for Tate. Braund never had a slip and Ranjitsinjhi, lame, occupied mid-on. We had no less than four men on the deep leg boundary for Braund, and if all four moved right across the ground for six singles in one over, when a left-handed batsman was in, each fieldsman would have covered some 1,200 yards in the over. It is always necessary to save not only your fieldsmen as much as possible, but also time. Tate had the very bad luck to do what all of us have done times without number, drop a catch which owing to the greatness of the occasion, advertised its costliness.

Yours faithfully,

A. C. MacLaren, Captain

Whatever the rights and wrongs of this debate it was considered purely academic at the time, for surely England could score the 124 needed for victory on the last day. Again there was overnight rain which prevented play until midday. The wicket was deteriorating with each passing minute so MacLaren changed his batting order, putting himself in to attack the bowling before lunch. With Abel he put on 36 by the interval, but who is to say that had Jessop been available, MacLaren would have missed the trick of sending him in for this crucial period and possibly clinching victory. When two wickets were down for 72 MacLaren, who had scored a forcing 35, looked up at the gathering storm clouds and decided that desperate measures were called for. He opened his shoulders to the next ball from Trumble, but alas, the towering drive was caught by Duff just inside the boundary. Afterwards Archie blamed himself for getting out but at 72 for two it would have been a defensive captain who did not take a chance to secure victory before the rain fell. The eventual outcome of the innings is history now: a collapse followed, including Clem Hill's miraculous catch on the boundary, leaving Fred Tate last man in with 8 to win. Delays for rain increased the tension, and after edging a boundary Tate was clean bowled and England had unbelievably lost. If anyone is to blame it is surely the selectors who put out a side without Jessop, Hirst or Haigh.

If the fourth Test has become famous then the story of the last one at the Oval has entered English folklore. Jessop's brilliant century and Hirst and Rhodes' 'We'll get'em in singles' partnership produced an even more exciting finish than at Old Trafford. The selectors came to their senses and restored Hirst and Jessop, banishing poor Fred Tate to the peace and contentment of county cricket. On a soft but true wicket Hirst at once showed his right to a place in the side by reducing Australia to 175 for seven, but a vital chance missed by Lilley proved expensive and the final score was 324. England's luck with the weather was out again, as heavy overnight rain produced a wicket tailor-made for Hugh Trumble whose eight wickets earned a lead of 141. George Hirst again embarrassed the selectors by top-scoring with 43, thereby avoiding the follow on.

Australia started their second innings with victory in sight, but in the first over disaster struck in the shape of Gilbert Jessop, the finest fielder of the day. Trumper played a ball into the covers but was sent back by Duff. The still damp turf caused him to slip and he was sitting on the pitch when Jessop's return ran him out. It was this single event more than anything else which turned the game England's way, according to MacLaren.

Even though Australia could score only 121 in this second innings, the wicket was playing all kinds of tricks and England's hopes of scoring 263 for victory looked slim. They appeared even slimmer when Saunders whipped out the first four in the order and the score stood at 48 for five. At this point Jessop joined Jackson and immediately began to hit. He was lucky, being missed twice before reaching 30, but he went on to score 104 out of 139 in seventy-five minutes—unique in Test cricket. The tail enders played their part, but it was Hirst (58 not out) and Rhodes (6 not out) who finally scored the 15 needed for the last wicket. It is perhaps a shame that they never said, 'We'll get'em in singles' and certainly the scorebook shows that this was not the case, but the result was fantastic enough not to need embellishment.

This brief description of the 1902 series shows above all that these were two great sides of virtually equal ability. The two desperately close games were one apiece and each could, and possibly should, have gone the other way. Given any luck with the weather England would certainly have balanced Australia's victory at Sheffield with a win in the Birmingham game. At the time the critics seemed to think that MacLaren had acquitted himself well as captain and was not to be blamed for defeat, but there were people in high places who did not share this view.

MacLaren felt that the selectors had robbed him of the series and writing many years later he had obviously not forgiven them. In one of his famous long sentences he wrote, 'I was a trifle sore that two of my selections for this match (the fourth) one of which was Jessop, were struck off my list forwarded to them at their request after I had informed them at a previous meeting that if they would play Jessop in every Test match, he would certainly run out Trumper from cover before the last game was played, as he chanced his wicket to this greatest cover in my time on two or three occasions in Australia. He was brought in too late for the Test game at the Oval and Trumper was almost at once run out by him. Let us hope that in the future the England captain will have the chief say in selection of teams against Australia and South Africa with assistance of cricketers of the day rather than the past.'

While these Test match dramas were being played out, Lancashire were experiencing a disappointing season and Archie was moderately quiet, finishing third in the batting averages. At the same time as Jessop was playing his phenomenal innings at the Oval, Lancashire were giving debuts to two new players at Brighton. One was Archie's younger brother, Geoffrey, who unfortunately could not emulate Archie's initial century on this ground twelve years earlier. In fact, in this and the subsequent match he scored only 0,3,3 and 1, the sum total of his first-class career. Being a MacLaren, however, his life was far from inconsequential or dull. At Harrow he represented the school at cricket, football and fives during this year of 1902, and by 1906 he was a police constable in South Africa. Six years later we find him captaining All Egypt in three unofficial 'Tests'. After being awarded the OBE during the First World War he became the Acting District Commissioner to Jerusalem in 1935.

The other, more significant, Lancashire debutant was Walter Brearley, the rumbustious amateur fast bowler whose ebullient career was to be so closely linked with MacLaren's over the next few years.

8
Sacked

During the winter Archie joined a London firm of wine merchants on the condition that the duties would not interfere with his cricket, and in 1903 he embarked on yet another full season as captain of Lancashire. Most of the early games were played on treacherous wickets in what was to prove a miserably wet summer but MacLaren again demonstrated his mastery of such conditions, starting with a magnificent 91 out of a total of 153 in the first match. Then, against Worcestershire, Lancashire won by an innings, thanks largely to a partnership of 233 in two and a half hours between MacLaren and F. H. Hollins of which Archie made 143. When the same Worcestershire bowlers journeyed to Aigburth for the return game, MacLaren was again at his very best, scoring another century in rapid time.

It was in late June when the news broke which constituted the most shattering reversal in Archie's entire cricketing career — another player had been chosen as captain of England over his head. To make matters worse his successor, P. F. Warner, despite his overseas experience on minor tours, had never played for England before and was not even the regular Middlesex captain. Not only MacLaren but also the entire English cricketing public were shocked and enraged at such apparent lunacy.

The story had really started during the winter when MacLaren had written to the Melbourne club suggesting a year's postponement of his proposed tour of Australia — from 1903–4 to 1904–5.

This was to have been another privately sponsored tour along the lines of his previous venture, and Archie's procrastination was not well received by the Australian cricket authorities or public. MacLaren's reasons were simply that he did not consider England's bowling strength to be good enough to win such a series, especially since he believed that the Yorkshire club would again take their parochial stand regarding Hirst and Rhodes. In addition he had sounded out Lockwood and Barnes, neither of whom would be able to tour. At one time the tour had been a definite possibility and MacLaren had even written to A. A. White, a leading umpire, inviting him to join the team in order to 'save the unpleasantness that arose last time over Crockett's incompetence'. Once he had changed his mind Archie simply imagined that a missive from him stating his intention to bring out a side in 1904–5 would be quite enough to keep the Australians happy. This naïvete proved his undoing as the Melbourne club predictably turned to the MCC requesting, via Warner, that they organise an alternative tour for the forthcoming season. One difficulty in the past regarding this procedure had been the absence of a representative governing body in Australia, but this was overcome and the MCC agreed to organise the tour, subject to its being able to raise a representative side. In effect, it was MacLaren's letter which initiated the arrangement that has stood to the present day.

The MCC captain chosen was Pelham Warner, F. S. Jackson having been the first choice until he declared himself unavailable quite early in the proceedings. MacLaren had been unequivocally passed over, a decision which rumour attributed largely to Lord Hawke and a certain dislike at Lord's of shamateurism. Throughout the rest of the summer the newspapers were full of rumour and counter-rumour as to who would accompany Warner to Australia, the main interest surrounding the leading amateurs, MacLaren and Fry. The latter kept the selectors waiting for several months while he tried to arrange employment as a journalist in Australia to help meet his expenses, and at the same time waged war in the *Daily Express* with regard to the plight of the impoverished amateur. In the end he was forced to decline the trip and Australia was never to see either Fry or Jackson.

MacLaren's position was even more confusing as throughout July he made a succession of curious statements to the press. First, at Tunbridge Wells he said he had yet to make up his mind whether to tour under Warner, then during the next game at the Oval he said that he definitely would not go, and that his decision was forced by a breach of cricket etiquette. A few days later when Middlesex, under Warner, visited Old Trafford it was 'officially' announced that Warner was quite willing to waive his own rights and go to Australia under MacLaren's captaincy. The following day this was strongly denied by Warner, who stated that in a private conversation he had told MacLaren that he would have played under him had he been elected captain by the MCC in the first place. It seems that MacLaren had chosen to misinterpret Warner's remarks and then leak them to the press. The public discussion was finally settled by an unusually frank statement from the MCC which confirmed Warner as their only choice as captain, and even went on to list in detail the financial terms for the tour and the status of various players' availability. In fact eight players, all amateurs, refused the offer to join the party—MacLaren, Jackson, Martyn, Palairet, Jessop, Dowson, Fry and Spooner. The professionals Hirst and Rhodes, however, were amongst the first to accept, with the benign blessing of Lord Hawke.

Throughout the controversy Warner had been pilloried in the popular press. *Cricket* newspaper entitled a profile of him 'The Most Abused Man of the Day', and reported that he was 'Condemned as an interloper and a nonentity'. Many of the more establishment figures, however, sided with the MCC: in a letter to *The Times* W. J. Ford marshalled the arguments against MacLaren by saying that he had 'no prescriptive rights of command', and that 'there are those who do not consider Mr MacLaren an ideal captain'. Another reason he suggested was, 'It is not unreasonable to pass over a captain whose bad luck has been the subject of frequent comment.' Finally he criticised MacLaren's decision not to play under Warner as 'not patriotic, and his excuse,

A LOT TO PONDER UPON.

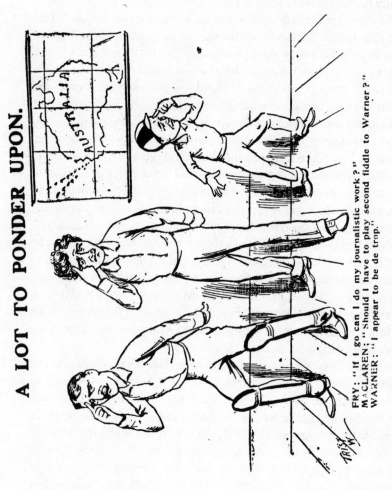

FRY: "If I go can I do my journalistic work?"
MacLAREN: "Should I have to play second fiddle to Warner?"
WARNER: "I appear to be de trop."

The summer of 1903 produced a tremendous controversy over the England team to tour Australia.

on the grounds of etiquette, a poor one. A certain form of pride is good, but there is such a thing as foolish pride.'

As the tour turned out Warner's appointment was a marvellous success and the MCC were thoroughly justified, but one cannot help feeling that the decision had not been based purely on cricketing grounds. MacLaren always claimed that Lord's had a 'down' on him, and no doubt this was a natural consequence of his sometimes abrasive manner and need to earn money from cricket.

Ironically, while this furore was raging MacLaren showed marvellous batting form, almost as if he were flaunting exactly what England would miss in Australia. His best innings of the season, and one of his greatest ever, was in the Gentlemen v. Players match at Lord's, a fixture which assumed the importance of a Test match in those days. Strangely enough MacLaren was selected as captain of the amateurs despite the fact that Warner was also in the team. Hayward won the toss for the Players, and with only Brearley able to take advantage of a slightly unsure wicket, they scored 387 for seven on the first day. They relied mainly on an innings of 139 by that holy cricketer, A. E. Knight who, on his first appearance in this match, probably secured his trip to Australia. The outcricket was poor and *The Times* was moved to comment reprovingly, 'The modern perfect wickets no doubt encourage bowling of a somewhat fantastic nature, but K. S. Ranjitsinjhi and Mr B. J. T. Bosanquet's leg break bowling is hardly of a class that should be seen in the great match of the season.' Within a few months Bosanquet's bowling was helping to recover the Ashes in Australia.

Next morning the last three wickets added 91 and by lunch Fry and Ranji were out for 39. Despite the loss of Barnes through injury after only one over, the amateurs could muster only 185 against Hargreave, Braund and Trott, and following on 293 behind they reached 74 for one by the close. Little excitement can have been expected from the last day, but in fact Lord's has rarely witnessed such memorable batting as that produced in the Gentlemen's second innings on a wicket taking some spin. In the first hour and a half Fry and Ranji added 142 before Ranji fell for 60, which could have been considerably more but for runs lost through his lameness. It was at this point that the real fireworks started. MacLaren marched out to join Fry, who was already in full flow, and immediately began to bat as if the best professional bowlers in the land were mere beginners. In the first hour after lunch 131 were scored and in all the pair added 309 in under three hours, before Archie had mercy and declared with an hour left. The score-card read as follows:

C. B. Fry	not out	232
P. F. Warner	c Hunter b Hargreave	27
K. S. Ranjitsinjhi	c Hunter b Gunn	60
A. C. MacLaren	not out	168
	b8, lb2, nb3	13

500 − 2 wkts dec.

This partnership has rightly entered the history of this famous fixture and ground. Wisden stated simply that 'The cricket they played was of a truly glorious description,' while Cardus averred that 'Never has such batsmanship been seen as this for opulence and prerogative.' C. B. Fry himself had the last word on MacLaren's innings and there can be no finer epigram: 'The crowd hardly noticed me. I batted in MacLaren's shadow.'

The season was a dismally wet one and on many occasions Archie was the only member of the Lancashire team to get any sort of score. One bright feature of the year, though, was the inception of the famous opening partnership of A. C. MacLaren and R. H. Spooner, the splendour of which was later immortalised by the pen of Sir Neville Cardus. Spooner had made his debut on leaving school in 1899 but for the next three years he was kept from cricket by military service in Ireland. Returning to Lancashire in 1903 he had a fine season culminating in an invitation, which he unfortunately had to decline, to join Warner's touring side. The undoubted highlight for MacLaren and Spooner in this or any other season was against Gloucestershire on the Aigburth ground at Liverpool, one

Maclaren in his early twenties: athletic, handsome, arrogant, at his peak as a batsman.

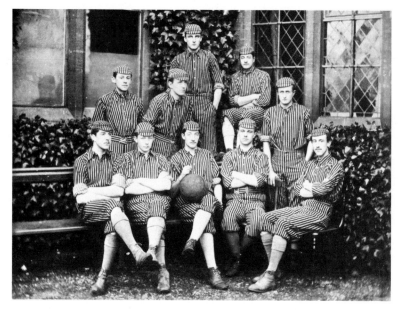

The Harrow soccer team of 1889 with Archie standing at the top.

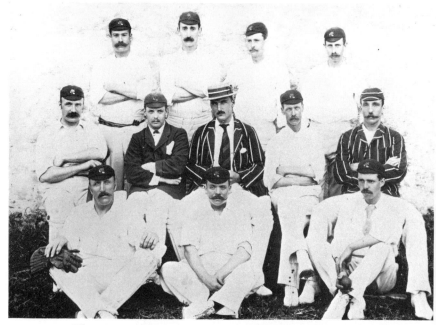

The Lancashire team photo for the match against Somerset, 16 July 1895, the day Maclaren scored his magnificent 424. *Top row:* Mold, Paul, Lancaster, Baker *Centre row:* Sugg, Benton, Maclaren, Tinsley, Ward (A) *Bottom row:* Smith (C), Briggs, Hallam.

The beautiful Maude, Archie's wife for almost fifty years, as she was when he first met her.

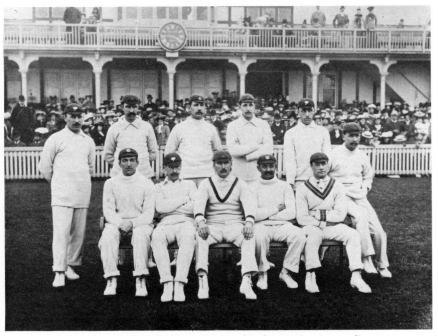

For many the greatest-ever England team (v. Australia at Birmingham in 1902) with Maclaren very much the leader. *Back row:* Hirst, Lilley, Lockwood, Braund, Rhodes, Tyldesley *Seated:* Fry, Jackson, Maclaren, Ranjitsinjhi, Jessop.

The Maclaren off drive as illustrated in *Great Batsmen: their methods at a glance*, by C. B. Fry & G. W. Beldam, published in 1905.

The straight drive demonstrated by Maclaren in the same book.

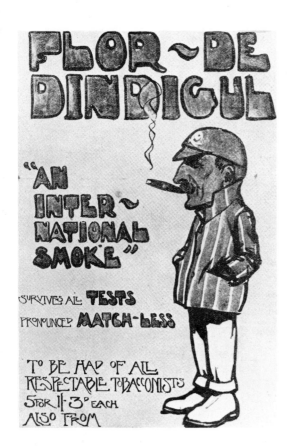

The famous Maclaren profile was even used to advertise cigars.

A photograph taken in 1906, one of the last of W. G. before his death. *Left to Right:* Ranji's son, Maclaren, W. G., Ranji, unknown.

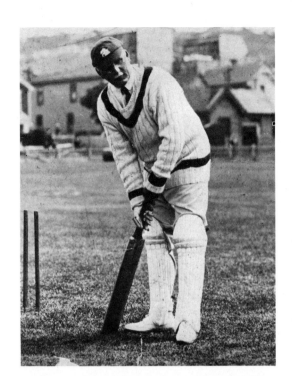

A posed photograph of Archie taken in New Zealand upon the completion of his final bow from first-class cricket – 200 not out against New Zealand on 1 January 1923.

The MCC team in Australia and New Zealand 1922–3. *Back row:* H. Tyldesley, C. H. Titchmarsh, T. C. Lowry, W. W. Hill-Wood *Centre row:* W. Ferguson (scorer), D. F. Brand, A. P. F. Chapman, J. F. Maclean, C. H. Gibson, A. P. Freeman *Front row:* R. J. Pope (medical adviser), A. C. Wilkinson, J. C. Hartley (Vice-Captain), A. C. Maclaren (Captain), F. S. G. Calthorpe, G. Wilson, H. D. Swan (Hon. Manager)

The team which beat the Australians at Eastbourne in 1921. *Back row:* G. Ashton, H. Ashton, A. P. F. Chapman, G. E. C. Wood, C. T. Ashton *Front row:* G. A. Faulkner, A. C. Maclaren, G. N. Foster, M. Falcon *On ground:* C. H. Gibson, W. Brearley not shown.

The old campaigner leaves the field for the last time.

of Archie's happiest hunting grounds. The batting of the pair on the first morning could not have been in more marked contrast to the miserably cold, overcast weather. In just three and a half hours they amassed 368 runs before Archie was caught behind for a memorable 204. Ten minutes later Spooner followed for 168 and by the close of play, despite the inevitable rain, the total was 474 for three. Further rain ruined the match but the opening stand remains a record for the county and was a highlight even amongst the great batting feats of the age.

Yet again this season some curious incidents can be recorded which would be so out of place in the game today. In a contest of massive scoring against Nottinghamshire at Trent Bridge the result was an inevitable draw after an innings of 247 from Spooner and two centuries by A. O. Jones. MacLaren himself bowled the last over of the day, stumps were drawn and the players walked off to the pavilion. John Gunn had been not out 49 so after some discussion the players returned, the stumps were pitched again and Eccles bowled one ball which enabled the batsman to reach 50. The other equally generous move by MacLaren came against Sussex at Brighton. In spite of a good start of 141 for the first wicket Ranji was in trouble at the start of his innings and had failed to score after thirty-five minutes at the wicket. The crowd became frustrated but were doubtless amazed when MacLaren put himself on to bowl and Ranji took six from the over; he then proceeded to play in his most fluent style for 144 not out. Surely this gesture was rather over-generous, even allowing for the great friendship between the pair; Ranji had recently been godfather to MacLaren's son.

This was a mixed season for Lancashire who finished fourth in the championship, as they had done the previous year. MacLaren at the age of thirty-two was a better and more effective batsman than ever before; as *Cricket* said, 'Mr MacLaren has quite got back his old form, and his old reputation as a man who is to be depended on for runs when no one could feel really confident of playing a long innings . . . never has he shown more conclusively that no England team can be called complete without him.'

But his vast ego had been dented by the decision of the MCC to pass him over as captain of England. Whether there was any animosity between the two men we cannot tell although Warner made a point of denying this at a dinner held at the Trocadero on the team's return. Certainly MacLaren never wrote disparagingly of Warner, in fact he rated the team's chances higher than did most critics and even gave Warner advice on team selection. On many occasions in later years, however, Warner, whilst praising MacLaren's batting and tactical awareness, still managed to devote many paragraphs to criticism of his overall leadership and personal qualities. It would come as no surprise to learn that Archie's rather overbearing attitude may have rankled with the sometimes over-sensitive Warner.

Passed over, then, but Archie was far from finished. The following season, 1904, was the very pinnacle of his career, with Lancashire winning the county championship for the only time under his captaincy. MacLaren was always basically a Test match player more than anything else, the everyday grind of county matches sometimes failing to hold his full concentration. During this year, though, Archie discovered a real zest for conducting Lancashire's triumphant campaign and he brought to bear all the tactical acumen and perception which he had displayed in the most vital Test match.

Archie opened the 1904 season with games for London County and the Rest of England whom he captained against Warner's victorious touring side. In a pre-season article in the *London Chronicle* MacLaren was far from optimistic about Lancashire's chances for the coming season considering the bowling to be weaker than formerly. In addition to the recent loss of Mold and Briggs, Barnes had now severed his fleeting connection with the county and Hallam had departed for Nottingham. Barnes had played only two full seasons for Lancashire before a disagreement over terms, and it has since become apparent that he would not even have stayed this long but for his respect for MacLaren as a captain.

Yet it was with this apparent lack of resources that the team struck a winning run which carried them through the season

undefeated and turned the county championship into a one-horse
race. The batting was, as always during MacLaren's reign,
immensely powerful with Spooner, Tyldesley, MacLaren,
Poidevin (an Australian over in England to study medicine), A. H.
Hornby (son of A.N.H.) and the double international, Jack Sharp.
The bowlers performed above all expectation with Hallows and
Cuttell each taking 100 wickets and Brearley and Kermode,
another Australian qualified from June, providing the cutting
edge.

The season started badly for Archie who missed three of the first
five games and was suffering greatly in the damp weather from
rheumatism. But the team had already set a furious pace by
winning six out of the first seven games and with the rest of the
summer mainly dry and sunny Archie soon returned to the helm.
Against Sussex at Old Trafford all the glories of the Golden Age
were on view for the fortunate spectators. On the last day Spooner
and MacLaren strode confidently to the wicket with the home side
needing quick runs for a declaration. In just two hours and ten
minutes they had achieved this task to the tune of 223 runs, both
players reaching a century before lunch – the first time this rare
double feat had been accomplished. As Cardus wrote, 'Has a
county possessed two batsmen who could begin an innings with
more than their appeal to the imagination?' The Saturday crowd
were then treated to a hundred by C. B. Fry and fifty from Ranji;
Manchester can rarely have witnessed such grandeur in a single
day. During the course of his innings Archie drove a ball clean out
of Old Trafford onto the railway line, but since the ball had bounced
just inside the ground only 4 runs were awarded. It is worth
remembering that throughout the major part of MacLaren's
career, and indeed that of the legendary Jessop, the ball had to clear
the confines of the ground for a six, the law remaining unchanged
until 1910.

Two more wins followed against Surrey and Kent and then came
a crushing victory over Somerset at Old Trafford. Dismissing the
West Country team for 166, the powerful Lancashire line-up cut
loose with no less than four men obtaining centuries in a total of

580. Johnny Tyldesley and MacLaren put on 187 in a hundred and five minutes with Archie crashing 151 in two and a quarter hours, 100 of which came in boundaries. It is easy to become blasé with the sheer monotony of recounting details of this season's run feasts, but the figures really speak for themselves. To show that their appetite for runs was far from sated, MacLaren and Tyldesley in the next game treated the frequenters of Trent Bridge to a partnership of 324 in a little over three hours. Their onslaught drove A. O. Jones, the Nottinghamshire captain, to adopt the then unheard of tactics of bowling wide of the leg stump with all the fielders on the leg side. Not that the bowlers were the only ones to suffer: one drive from MacLaren hit Tyldesley on the chest, laying him out for several minutes.

At this stage, around the middle of the season, the team produced a decisive charge of six successive wins which effectively decided the championship. Their record was now an impressive played 19, won 15, lost 0. A temporary halt was applied by Yorkshire in George Hirst's benefit match at Leeds. The home team made a mockery of MacLaren's decision to put them in on a wet wicket by scoring 403, and the first defeat of the season appeared likely when Hirst himself shot out MacLaren, Spooner and Tyldesley for just 4 runs. Following on 230 behind, with the wicket playing all sorts of tricks, MacLaren set about denying his only championship rivals the crucial points. The final second innings total of 163 for three which achieved this end appears to have owed much to Tyldesley's brilliant 108 not out, but the correspondent of the *Manchester Guardian* had eyes only for MacLaren: 'Tyldesley's not out century was for once overshadowed by a remarkable innings in which only 5 runs were scored—the innings of MacLaren. Never, surely, has the Lancashire captain made a more supreme effort for his side than that of today. If he had failed then probably not all the lives given to Tyldesley would have availed to save Lancashire. But MacLaren played an innings of a lifetime—splendid to watch for the beautiful perfection of his batsmanship, and magnificently inspiring because of the fine purpose behind it all. For an hour he faced all the bowling strength that

Yorkshire could command, although he only scored two singles at the end of that hour.' MacLaren's five singles in an hour and a half certainly was 'an innings of a lifetime' since it was far and away the slowest of his career, but against the dangerously biting and lifting deliveries of Hirst and company it was vital.

The closing weeks of the season, which were played without Brearley or Hallows, showed a distinct falling off in the side's fortunes but they managed to remain unbeaten and the title was settled. The chief factor, unusual in the championship winners, was the rapid rate at which runs were scored. MacLaren had captained brilliantly, but although he had batted devastatingly at times, the more perceptive critics detected a slight falling off from his younger days. With the advancing years Archie was becoming increasingly susceptible to poor health and injury and he often played when not fully fit.

This year, 1904, MacLaren made a rare appearance at the Scarborough Festival, joining in the holiday fun with an innings of 114 in eighty-five minutes for MCC against his old friends, Yorkshire. The end of the season was soured somewhat by the first of many disagreements between Walter Brearley and the Lancashire club, notably the President, A. N. Hornby. Brearley had been left out of the team to play against the Rest of England and he reacted with a threat to play the following season with London County rather than Lancashire. The matter resolved itself, as it always did with Brearley, but not without the following pointed piece of snobbery from Hornby regarding Brearley's background, 'It is obvious that no man can be an accomplished player and know how to conduct himself unless he is either an ''old boy'' or an ''old blue''.'

During the winter Archie journeyed with Ranji to India and had a memorable time riding elephants and hunting tigers. Ranji had recently appointed MacLaren his personal assistant, and although the position was not a complete sinecure, doubtless the always-generous Prince saw it as an opportunity to relieve his old friend's financial struggles. In later years Ranji also helped to finance the education of Archie's two sons; both followed their father's footsteps at Elstree and Harrow.

Archie returned to England shortly before the arrival of the 1905 Australians. The forthcoming series was keenly awaited, a chief talking point being the England captaincy for which there were three logical candidates – Warner, MacLaren and Jackson. Of these, Jackson had been unavailable when considered the first choice two years previously but he now declared his readiness to play during the summer. The establishment's disapproval of MacLaren persisted, so the committee of J. A. Dixon, Hawke and Warner elected Jackson captain of his country for the first and only time. The appointment was not universally popular, but the subsequent success story has now become legendary and has even been the subject of an entire book by Alan Gibson.

The contrast between results under Jackson and MacLaren is amazing considering that the England team was much the same as in 1902, but the luck ran exclusively England's way in 1905 and the Australian side was inferior to the previous combination. Indeed, Darling's team were written off by the public before ever a match was played. Hugh Trumble still at the height of his powers, Jones and Saunders, whose actions were suspect, were omitted from the team amidst great controversy. Feeling in Australia ran so high that a public subscription was raised with the intention of privately sponsoring Saunders and others to strengthen the weak bowling resources. This offer was predictably rejected and the main hopes of the side were pinned on Tibby Cotter, an erratic successor to Jones with a slinging delivery like that of Jeff Thomson. It is also interesting to note that many in Australia considered Marsh, an aborigine who had not played first-class cricket for two years, to be the best bowler in the country, but he was excluded from the team apparently because of colour prejudice.

With Test match duration still limited to three days in England, and considering the Australian batting strength, the likelihood was that the astute and experienced Darling would at least be able to make a draw of most games even if he did not have the bowling needed to force victory. In the event, despite England's overwhelming advantage in winning all five tosses, the weak Australian team came much closer to a complete stalemate than is often realised. Any luck that was available ran exclusively England's way, as it had always refused to do under MacLaren. In both of England's victories heavy rain fell before the players had even left the field and would certainly have prevented further play.

The outcome of the toss had almost been decided before the season started since Lord Harris proposed an unsuccessful motion to the MCC that the Laws should incorporate a method of alternate choice of innings. This idea had first been mooted by MacLaren in Australia in 1901 and was later taken up by Jessop.

Archie himself started the season in fine form having returned from India at the end of March. A useful 48 for the Gentlemen against the Australians was followed by 90 in a hundred minutes and 63 not out against Leicestershire, his usual early season victims, on the usual poor wicket. He then journeyed confidently to Trent Bridge for the first Test of the summer, but on a hard fast wicket England succumbed miserably to Laver (seven for 64) for a mere 196 which allowed Australia to gain a first innings lead of 25. Although the gentle pace of Laver had done most damage it was the fierce attack of Tibby Cotter which rattled the top half of the English batting order. Even seventy years ago voices were raised at the way in which he repeatedly pitched short and sent the ball whistling past the batsmen's ears. On the second morning the outcome of the match, and probably the series, rested on how well the English batsmen could recover their composure and assert some sort of authority over Cotter in the second innings. It perhaps reflects the spirit of this era that Jackson's answer was to promote MacLaren from number four to number one in order to 'take the bull by the horns' as C. B. Fry put it. Sir Neville Cardus has portrayed beautifully the mood of MacLaren just before he went out to bat at 12.25 on Friday afternoon. The young Cardus apparently witnessed Archie striding along the pavilion corridor muttering to himself, 'Cotter! I'll bloody Cotter him!' Whether true or apocryphal we shall never know but as Cardus once wrote in justification, 'It certainly observes the highest order of truth which is truth to character.'

The result of this bold move was that the old firm of Hayward and MacLaren frustrated the Australians just as they had in 1901–2. With the Surrey man playing for keeps, Archie tore into Cotter, Laver and McLeod, forcing Darling to resort to Warwick Armstrong's ultra-defensive leg theory for the first of many occasions on the tour. The pair had put on 145 in two and a half hours when Hayward departed for 47, and in so doing they had laid the bogey of Cotter on the fastest wicket he would encounter all summer. After Archie had reached his century he began to hit out recklessly as tiredness caught up with him, and he was eventually caught in the deep for 140 out of 222 for two. This was surprisingly his only Test century in England and was the highest of the five he scored altogether. The tone had been set for the entire series and the Australian bowling, so devastating in the first innings, was never to recover the initiative; Darling was forced into a policy of containment. All the Australian plans to curb MacLaren by keeping the ball away from what they considered his best shots, the off drive and cut, had been destroyed by a succession of brilliant leg-side pulls and glances.

During the course of Archie's great innings he was incensed by Armstrong's leg theory bowling and made no attempt to disguise his feelings. At times he just kicked at the ball as it passed wide of the leg stump and when Hayward was facing he just sat back on his bat handle at the non-striker's end. These antics encouraged the crowd to hoot and jeer the Australians, and several times Armstrong stopped in the middle of his run-up until the noise subsided.

Despite this marvellous innings and useful supporting knocks by Jackson and Tyldesley, a result must have seemed a remote possibility when the declaration left Australia only five hours to obtain the 402 needed. At 60 for one a draw was certain and F. S. Jackson was on the point of changing the bowling when MacLaren is said to have approached the captain between overs with the advice, 'Keep Bosie on a little longer'. The result was eight for 107 for Bosanquet's leg breaks and googlies and an easy win for England. Fortune had certainly smiled on England; rain began to fall immediately the game was over. Furthermore, Vic Trumper was unable to bat properly in either innings due to a back strain received when diving for a slip catch.

England's clear superiority was demonstrated again in the Lord's match although a result was impossible as the whole of the last day was lost to rain. On a difficult wicket MacLaren led England's first innings tactics of squeezing out as many runs as possible with a defensive innings of 56 in two and a half hours. Thanks to this and similar fighting efforts from Fry and Tyldesley a first innings lead of 107 was earned and the time had come for different tactics. MacLaren dealt with the difficult batting conditions with consummate skill and his brilliantly stroked 79 had put England in a winning position when the heavens opened. This effort of Archie's was easily the highlight of the match and was considered one of his finest innings in England.

Archie missed the third match of the series through injury and he did not really recover his best health or form for the remainder of the season. Although he scored as many as thirteen fifties this year his 140 in the first Test was his only century. Archie always maintained that a cricketer was past his best when over thirty years old and it appears that, while he had lost none of his brilliance, his general fitness was beginning to decline. The natural consequence of this was his failure to build any long innings out of a succession of good starts.

He returned for the final two Tests of the series but contributed little with the bat. The Old Trafford match provided the second English victory of the series and again everything ran Jackson's way. After England had made a big score on the first day overnight rain produced a venomous wicket on which Australia were forced to follow on. Gradually on the second day the wicket dried and rolled out well so that by the close a draw looked likely at 118 for one. But rain again came to England's aid to produce a real 'sticky' on Saturday and the last nine wickets tumbled for a mere 51. Immediately after the fall of the last wicket the heavens opened again for the remainder of the last day, and Joe Darling could have been forgiven for thinking that the infamous Manchester climate was completely at Jackson's command.

H. S. Altham in his *History of Cricket* summed up as follows: 'That we won the rubber on our merits cannot be doubted, but it is equally certain that the Australians had the worst of the luck, and played a long way below form in some of the Test cricket.' F. S. Ashley-Cooper stated that Darling's team was the weakest touring side since 1893 and F. S. Jackson himself conceded, 'I know of no other occasion on which the luck played so unfair a part as it had during the two seasons when Mr MacLaren captained the English side, just as it has been unfairly kind to myself this year.'

What then of the fascinating comparison of Jackson and MacLaren as captains? There are basically two schools of thought. The first, which held sway with a section of the public at the time, was that MacLaren should have been England's captain by right, and that his experience of three tours to Australia gave him an unrivalled knowledge of Test match strategy. The other view, more widely held especially with hindsight, was that Jackson could get the best out of his team despite MacLaren's abilities as a tactician. In addition there is the obvious contrast in the two captains' share of luck. Perhaps this series produced the ideal combination: Jackson as captain to unify the team and get the best out of individuals and MacLaren as deputy to spot tactical and strategical subtleties, especially weaknesses in the opposition. Jackson certainly acknowledged Archie's contribution: 'MacLaren in all ways acted as partner rather than lieutenant in the command.' In fact he took over the captaincy of the side when Jackson was bowling and he always accompanied the skipper on wicket inspections. The only matter on which the two parted company was that of team selection, both being members of the committee. MacLaren as always advocated the choice of Jessop but Jackson's opposite view held sway. Jackson summed up the relationship: 'It was scarcely an enviable position for any man who was at all sensitive to be practically superceded, but MacLaren played as a cricketer and as a true sportsman.'

The season for Lancashire was a slight disappointment after the championship win, especially since MacLaren had led them to eight wins in the first ten games. With MacLaren, Spooner,

Tyldesley and Brearley all playing for England later in the season, they could not keep it up and were, as so often, pipped by Yorkshire for the title.

The match with Sussex at Brighton managed to throw up the usual MacLaren controversy. Lancashire batted and were 364 for five by the end of the first day including a rapid 92 from Archie himself. At lunch on the second day the score had reached a massive 587 for eight but the expected declaration was not forthcoming and for some odd reason MacLaren batted on. C. B. Fry, the Sussex captain, showed his disgust by ordering C. L. A. Smith and H. P. Chaplin to bowl underhand daisy-cutters until the innings was eventually closed at 601 for eight. Despite bowling Sussex out for 383 Lancashire did not enforce the follow on, but batted again to reach 302 for six against the part-time bowlers. MacLaren did not make an appearance on the last day.

On a happier note for Archie the season closed with news that the Lancashire committee were opening a testimonial fund for him with a contribution from the club of £250. By October the fund had reached £816 3s 6d and at Archie's request part of it was to be used to purchase 'a memento of his long association with amateur cricket'. Shortly afterwards the Lancashire committee minutes recorded that on 8 December MacLaren resigned the captaincy for business reasons although he hoped to continue playing in the important games. The committee implored him to reconsider and two weeks later Archie withdrew his resignation with the proviso that he would have to miss certain 'minor' matches.

9
Decline

The years that followed were ones of gradual decline for Archie who was now in his mid-thirties. Although he retained the captaincy of Lancashire until 1907, he was beginning to feel the strain and missed an increasing number of matches. Not that he lost any enthusiasm for the game and on occasion, usually when runs were most needed, he still batted with all his old fluency and majesty. His old enemy, rheumatism, was more of a handicap than ever, and the need to secure an income with which to bring up his two young sons became more and more pressing. For these reasons his appearances gradually became less frequent.

The first game at Old Trafford in 1906, against Warwickshire, was the occasion for A. N. Hornby to present MacLaren with the proceeds from his testimonial fund. The memento took the form of a hall clock, a diamond necklace for Mrs MacLaren and a handsome cheque. In his speech of thanks Archie announced that the money would be used for the purchase of a car to facilitate the journey from Knutsford, where the family were now living. In those days not everybody shared Archie's enthusiasm for motor cars and a number of subscribers to the testimonial fund were extremely annoyed. True to character, however, MacLaren showed scant regard for their opinion and duly told them he would do as he liked with his money. The difference of opinion became public knowledge very quickly and even gave rise to the following lines of doggerel:

112

To Archie MacLaren quoth Spooner,
'I'm thinking of buying a schooner.'
Said Archie, 'What rot! When a motor I've got,
We can get to the cricket ground sooner.'

The Warwickshire match was unfortunately ruined by a typically soft Old Trafford wicket which caused twenty-four wickets to
fall in four and three-quarter hours play on the first day. Archie
stood head and shoulders over the rest of the players, top-scoring in
the game with 58 not out as well as hitting 23 in a first innings total
of only 76. Throughout the rest of May, Lancashire met a succession of poor wickets so Archie's scores were low; all the same they
were usually higher than anybody else's. Due partly to rheumatism, business calls and even perhaps disillusionment, Archie
missed many games in June and July including the centenary
Gentlemen v. Players match in which Fielder took all ten wickets
in an innings. Somehow the atmosphere was not quite the same—as
well as MacLaren's absences very little was seen of Walter
Brearley.

It was not until 23 July that MacLaren returned to lead his
county, appropriately enough at Lord's, with Middlesex providing
the opposition. The pitch provided yet another bowler's wicket and
Lancashire suffered a heavy defeat. Nobody dealt better with the
conditions than Archie who called on all his experience to score 35
and 38 out of two pitiful Lancashire totals. By the time Middlesex
batted a second time they required only 81 for victory but even this
score was far from trivial on such a difficult pitch. Yet MacLaren
showed no inclination to make the task unduly difficult, allowing
Poidevin to bowl eight assorted overs of experimental googlies for
50 runs. Such a 'faint-hearted policy', as *Cricket* magazine called
it, was the season's example of the occasional aberration to which
Archie was prone when someone or something had ruffled his
feathers. It was no coincidence that such an event often occurred at
Lord's. The statement, 'Lord's is the place where plots are
hatched,' once appeared in an article under MacLaren's name in
the *Sun* although it had in fact been written by G. Beldam. The

mistake apparently occurred because Ranjitsinhji had been made editor for the day and was experiencing difficulty in obtaining enough material. The sentiments may have been MacLaren's but he was livid that they should appear in print, knowing only too well the harm it could do him.

For the rest of the season MacLaren had a wretched time with a succession of low scores and dropped catches. Everything seemed to be going wrong and he missed the last few matches, finishing the season with a top score of only 61. The one promising event of that year occurred at the nets one day when Archie was trying to get some much-needed batting practice. An unlikely-looking youngster was hanging around the net and during a lull in the proceedings he bowled a few left-arm swervers at the great man. Archie's immediate reaction was to announce, 'I'll take that boy to Leicester with me.' That boy was named Harry Dean who proceeded to take a hundred wickets the following season, over 1,200 wickets in his career and to play for England!

During the winter Archie was again in India with Ranji and Sir Arthur Priestley, and it became clear that he would be taking even more of a back seat in 1907. In November he requested that he should not be elected to the Lancashire committee as planned, then on 27 January the club received the following communication: 'It will be impossible for me to play quite so regularly as previously. I shall hope to manage three days a week and if the committee considers that sufficient to justify my retention of the captaincy I shall be pleased to continue the same.' In mid-March the committee were informed that because of MacLaren's recent illness he would have to go away and miss the opening of the new season. Archie was actually in India with Ranji until the middle of June and it was not until the 24th of that month that he resumed the county captaincy. In his second match, against Derbyshire at Chesterfield, he appeared to be back to his best with scores of 47 and 92 but he could not sustain this form. Lancashire were struggling under the prolonged absences of Spooner, Brearley and Cuttell.

Then, on 22 July, the county team travelled south to Lord's for a match which was to prove controversial even by MacLaren standards—again, let it be noted, at the headquarters of cricket's establishment. Heavy rains on the first day, Monday, delayed play until 2.45pm when MacLaren and Spooner began a Lancashire innings together for the first time that season. By the time further rain had forced the players off at five o'clock the total was 57 for one, MacLaren 27 not out. On Tuesday morning the pitch was found to be under water and the umpires, Flowers and Marlow, soon adjudged that no play would be possible. When the decision was announced a handful of spectators decided to walk out to the wicket to look for themselves, and then proceeded to make a protest in front of the pavilion. A potentially unruly scene was soon pacified by the authorities who ruled that the spectators would be allowed free passes for the next day's play. So far, so good.

At this point MacLaren dropped a bombshell in the form of the following statement issued to the press: 'Owing to the pitch having been deliberately torn up by the public, I, as captain of the Lancashire eleven, cannot see my way to continue the game, the groundsman bearing me out that the wicket could not be again put right.' This decision was made by MacLaren on the Tuesday afternoon and was of course completely outside the laws of the game. The umpires were the sole arbiters of whether the pitch was fit but they seem to have succumbed to Archie's authoritative manner. The outcome was that Lancashire did not appear on Wednesday and the match was drawn, but the arguments raged on for weeks. The Middlesex captain, Gregor MacGregor, disagreed with MacLaren's action and R. D. Walker, the Middlesex president, stated in *The Field* that on Wednesday the pitch had rolled out almost perfectly. W. G. Grace in the *Morning Post* and P. F. Warner in the *Westminster Gazette* lent their weight to the almost unanimous condemnation of Archie's precipitous action.

There is little doubt that Archie's action was unjustified and high-handed but there was more to this than awkwardness. MacLaren had not seen eye to eye with the MCC/Lord's establishment since the arguments over the 1901–2 and 1903–4 tours to Australia. He felt that they had a down on him and he always used to say that he would get 'six of the best if I used the wrong door at

Lord's.' Ironically, in June of this year 1907, Archie had been asked to lead the forthcoming touring party to Australia, an invitation he had to refuse because of his Indian commitments. Archie always had something of an inferiority complex because he could not really afford to live like a member of the landed gentry. His high-handed attitudes, such as in the Middlesex match, were part of his general over-compensation which made him appear awkward at times.

As usual the only effect all this criticism and controversy had on MacLaren was a galvanising one: in the very next match after the Lord's affair, Archie cocked a snook at his detractors by scoring 107 in a low scoring victory over Warwickshire at Old Trafford. Although the conditions were far from ideal MacLaren was determined to do well. It took him nearly four hours of grim resolution, the slowest century he ever made in England. This was the first time he had topped the hundred mark for two years and when he left the field, exhausted, he was a satisfied man.

Sadly, the rest of the season fizzled out rather unremarkably for Archie. Lancashire finished a disappointing sixth and it became clear that the great man's reign as captain was virtually over. His duties with Ranji were more and more time-consuming. Typically Archie had no illusions about his failing powers and it was very much his own decision to take a back seat. He was overweight, sorely troubled by rheumatism and convinced that his place should go to a younger man. It was one such, A. H. Hornby, the son of the great A.N., who took over the leadership for 1908 but the committee and public were still keen for Archie to play whenever possible and in late June of that year they welcomed him back to the team with open arms. The vast experience and knowledge of the older man were invaluable to Hornby but MacLaren's batting made little impact. After only seven matches he dropped out for the rest of the season.

There was, however, one truly memorable occasion that summer of 1908 when the years were rolled back and some of the old glory momentarily returned. For some years the Gentlemen v. Players match at the Oval had become something of a poor relation to the game at Lord's, but this year an effort was made to restore its quality. Two fine sides were collected and Archie was nominated captain of the amateurs who also included the likes of Fry, Ranji and Warner. The wicket was far from perfect and the Players could find no answer to the fearsome pace of Neville Knox who took seven for 52 in his first game of the season. The Gentlemen would scarcely have fared any better but for a marvellous partnership between MacLaren and Fry which, for many present at the ground, must have stirred the memory of this pair's famous assault in the Lord's fixture five years previously. For just one and three-quarter hours those memories sprang to life as 141 runs were added in a third-wicket stand which effectively won the game. Their play showed the perfect economy of effort only brought about by experience. The newspaper *Cricket* noted, 'A. C. MacLaren overshadowed Fry and gave more than a glimpse of his old form.' In the second innings the fortunate spectators were presented with another cameo of former days as MacLaren and Ranji shared a fine partnership before Archie made the winning hit.

MacLaren's other partnership with Ranji, his position as the Prince's secretary, was also in the news later in the year. A furious Archie found himself summoned to the Guildford County Court for non-payment of the Jam of Nawanagar's rates on Shillinglee Park, a property Ranji had rented for the year. Despite a protest and an appeal by Archie it was ruled that as secretary he (and not his employer) was liable for payment. Archie's vigorous defence that, as a ruling Prince, Ranji was exempt from rates unfortunately carried little weight with the magistrates.

The following summer of 1909 brought an unexpected fillip to MacLaren's cricket career which had appeared to be gradually fading away. The reason, as so often in the past, was yet another meeting with Australia, the 'enemy' whom he respected and admired so much. For Archie these Test matches were the only kind of cricket which he found completely fulfilling and challenging. Consequently while the football season was still holding the public's attention, the *Daily Mail* reported: 'A. C. MacLaren is working hard to get into proper trim and if he can only satisfy himself there can be little doubt that he will so satisfy the selection committee that he will be one of the first choices—indeed the first choice—if F. S. Jackson cannot find time to play. Players and public alike are clamouring for the return of A. C. MacLaren who is perhaps the greatest captain England has ever had though F. S. Jackson is more adept at spinning the coin and winning the toss.'

In early May the selectors, Lord Hawke, C. B. Fry and H. D. G. Leveson-Gower, duly asked Jackson to captain England in the forthcoming series. Owing to other commitments he was forced to decline the invitation, and he had in fact scarcely played at all since the victorious 1905 season. The public and critics alike were unanimous in their opinion that MacLaren was the natural next choice. In spite of poor batting form of late and repeated attacks of ill health, nobody at the time would have suggested that even Fry or Warner could be considered before MacLaren. F. S. Ashley-Cooper announced the appointment as 'a matter of rejoicing' and, whatever Archie's recent form, it was argued that he had been successfully recalled many times before with little or no practice behind him.

The cricket public were in buoyant mood and although the last MCC team had been heavily defeated in Australia the press confidently predicted success for MacLaren. The Australians no longer had the powerful bowling of Trumble, Jones or Saunders, nor the batting of Hill and Darling. The left-handed replacements for these last two, Bardsley and Ransford, had not achieved any reputation as yet and the name of Macartney hardly instilled the respect that it was to do in later years. The tourists started the season, a very wet one, in wretched form struggling to hold their own even against the county sides.

MacLaren was in good batting form in Lancashire's early season matches but was forced to miss the MCC v. Australians match which preceded the first Test. He had been confined to bed with a heavy cold but it was announced that on no account would he miss the Test at Birmingham. Archie was invited by the three selectors to discuss the team but shortly afterwards Lord Hawke, the chairman, was forced to go to France for three weeks on account of his health. Nevertheless, he left behind him a strong, well-balanced team for the vital first encounter. The final XI could only conceivably have been strengthened by the inclusion of Hayward who was unfit, Brearley who was ruled out by the very wet conditions and poor footholds, and Barnes who was only getting practice in the leagues. The fielding of a comparatively old side was strengthened by the vital presence of Jessop, Hobbs and Jones.

As was usual in pre-war days the first Test of the season started at the end of May. Unfortunately there was still plenty of rain about and the first day's play was limited to forty-five minutes during which Australia scored 22 for two, Bardsley falling to a superb slip catch by MacLaren. Next morning on a wicket which was never vicious Australia were dismissed by Hirst and Blythe for 74. England fared little better with 121 and by the close the opposition's second innings stood at 67 for two. The last morning's play was therefore crucial but, thanks again to Hirst and Blythe, Australia could set England a target of only 105 for victory. *The Times* noted that MacLaren's astute field placing was a feature of the English outcricket and the catches by A. O. Jones and J. Tyldesley were considered almost unbelievable. The 105 needed could have proved embarrassing on this pitch but Archie decided to demote himself and open instead with Hobbs and Fry, both of whom had been dismissed first ball the day before. This proved an inspired decision as the runs were scored without loss in only ninety minutes with Hobbs especially showing marvellous skill in the way he dealt with the turning ball. England had made a successful start, leaving the Australians contemplating their woeful batting and lack of bowling penetration.

The second Test at Lord's has become infamous for the curious and controversial selection of the England team. With Hawke still out of the country the final nomination of fourteen players was in the hands of Fry and Leveson-Gower. Although this pair had consulted with MacLaren, the absence of Jessop and Brearley indicated that little notice was taken of his views. Public criticism was unanimous, particularly in the case of Jessop who Wisden claimed was 'the one indispensable player'. Perhaps more important though

was the enforced exclusion of Blythe who was suffering from nervous strain brought on by the first Test. A doctor stated that Blythe
did not suffer in this way from a county match but that a Test
match was too much for his sensitive nature. It was hoped that after
a few weeks rest he would be available for the later matches. This
was a considerable blow to England as Blythe was the most effective
bowler in the country at this time. The team which finally took the
field was totally unbalanced; the bowling was in the hands of Hirst,
Haigh, King and Relf, all four of whom were medium pacers, while
King played mainly as a batsman. The selectors were quite properly slated in the press but who exactly was responsible? Leveson-
Gower and Warner, neither of whom could get on with MacLaren,
tried to imply that these selectorial decisions were the captain's but
there is considerable evidence to show that this was untrue. In a
letter to Jessop, George Beldam, while lamenting the poor team
selection, mentioned that 'he [Archie] can't apparently have his
own way! He wanted Thomas Jayes [the Leicestershire fast bowler]
but Haigh was given him!' Another letter to Jessop, this one from
MacLaren, also indicated that both Jessop and Brearley would have
been in Archie's team: 'You know at any rate the value I place on
your presence on the England side, and it bucks me up to think you
will be with us at Leeds . . . Brearley could have played but would
not when I saw him before the game – his bag being at Tonbridge
but he would not wire for it.' MacLaren had asked Brearley to play
at 11.15 on the morning of the match although he was not in the
original squad. According to Leveson-Gower he preferred to stand
outside the boxes at Lord's and give a loud and prolonged account
of why he should be playing.

The team was further hampered by the inclusion of Hayward
whose leg was by no means fully fit. This choice was presumably
due to the last minute withdrawal of Fry, but it resulted in Hayward
missing a running catch and being run out in the second innings.
All in all the team was a shambles of 'blunders in which it is universally believed Mr MacLaren had no share' according to the
Liverpool Post. The bowling line-up left much to be desired – 'rash'
according to *The Times* – but it was England's feeble batting that

was to cost them the game. Noble had the best of a soft wicket after asking England to bat first and Australia secured a lead of 81; Ransford, who was the mainstay with an innings of 143, was dropped at 13, 56 and 61. The fact that one of these chances went to MacLaren is always given far more emphasis by his critics than the fact that Trumper was missed on nought, that A. O. Jones, the finest of fielders, also dropped a chance and that countless runs were stolen owing to the absence of Jessop. It seemed that as the season wore on, and indeed in later years, many people were only too pleased for such an opportunity to denigrate MacLaren. Many of those who had been on the receiving end of Archie's abrasive manner were now preparing to sit back for the last laugh at his expense.

To return to Lord's in 1909, England's bowlers fared better than expected; 'MacLaren handled the bowling at his command with considerable skill,' according to F. S. Ashley-Cooper, and only a reasonable batting display was required on the last day to secure a draw. Disastrously, the first six men fell for 41 and although MacLaren and Jones doubled the score, the final total was not enough to stave off a humiliating defeat. Amidst the wholesale condemnations that followed it was generally agreed that MacLaren had received the only genuinely unplayable ball of the entire innings.

By now MacLaren had had enough and on Lord Hawke's return from France he offered to resign the captaincy and drop out from the remaining three matches. But Hawke had a steadying influence on affairs and persuaded MacLaren to continue and even managed to restore sanity to the selection of the team. The redoubtable quintet of Jessop, Fry, Rhodes, Brearley and Syd Barnes were restored to the side much to everyone's relief, and another of Archie's personal favourites, Jack Sharp, was given a trial. MacLaren's waning enthusiasm was even boosted to the extent of seeking practice in a match for MCC against Grantham and District. In this game he scored 94 and 24 not out but for Lancashire his form was no better than in the Tests.

'We can and will beat them with ordinary luck,' wrote MacLaren before the vital third Test at Leeds but alas, even ordinary luck was more than fate had in store. With the match barely an hour old disaster struck when Jessop strained himself so badly in the field that he was taken away in an ambulance, destined to remain on the sidelines for the remainder of the season. The bowling of Barnes and the batting of the Lancashire pair, Tyldesley and Sharp, kept England in contention until the last innings when they collapsed from 60 for two to 87 all out. This latest batting debacle caused more public outrage and even *The Times* began to query MacLaren's position: 'No fault can be found with Mr MacLaren as a captain; his management of the bowling and disposition of the field has all along been admirable, but Mr MacLaren is not as young as he was, is not always in the best of health, and has not shown his best batting form this or even last year.'

It was clearly the batting that was letting England down and MacLaren was moved to write in the *Daily Dispatch*: 'We have a bad batting side; in fact it is the worst batting team that England has had for many years.' He then went on to attempt a rather unsuccessful rationalisation of his own position: 'I foresaw the trouble, I did not want to be the captain. My cricket career is coming to a close, and I realised that these tests would not do my reputation as a leader any good. However, I have had to play in spite of my personal wishes.' Archie was clearly concerned that the team's deficiencies were rubbing off on him; he also sought to ensure that he would not be implicated in any more selectorial mishaps. In the *Athletic News* he wrote, 'I sincerely hope that the selection committee will not make too many changes in the next team. I am afraid that they will.' With Hobbs and Jessop injured three new batsmen were called up, namely Spooner, Hutchings and Warner, and, with Blythe available again, comment was generally favourable. The match itself was ruined by rain and with the Ashes at stake Noble rightly refused to set England any sort of target on the last afternoon, a decision which in those days was regarded as somewhat shabby.

Finally, with the Ashes already retained by Australia, the teams came to the Oval where they at last played on a good wicket and in favourable weather. This was to be MacLaren's last Test match and he probably knew it, but controversy and criticism followed him to the very end. In the words of *Wisden*, 'A fatal blunder was committed...a blunder for which it was generally understood MacLaren was responsible. Experts occasionally do strange things and this was one of the strangest...touches the confines of lunacy.' 'Betrayed England to Australia.' These and similar comments followed the announcement on the morning of the match that Buckenham, the Essex fast bowler, was to be omitted from the England team. On a hard, fast wicket the bowling was to be in the hands of Barnes and D. W. Carr, plus four all-rounders including the redoubtable Rhodes; Blythe was also excluded. Carr, a 37-year-old googly bowler who had only made his first-class debut a few weeks previously, was included after some success for the Gentlemen v. Players. While he was regarded as something of a secret weapon, the absence of a fast bowler was the signal for a torrent of criticism aimed particularly at MacLaren, who was apparently responsible for the decision.

After Noble had won the toss for the fifth successive time the justification for this criticism was not long in coming. MacLaren opened the bowling with Carr, on whose ageing shoulders so much rested, and for a time the gamble proved successful. Operating from the Vauxhall end Carr took three wickets in his first seven overs to leave the Australians reeling at 58 for four. Archie's winning streak did not continue, though, and the lack of another front-line bowler was one gamble which was doomed to failure. Bardsley and Trumper, followed by Macartney, at first halted Carr's progress then mercilessly destroyed his once impressive bowling analysis. MacLaren, embarrassed by the slim resources at his command, was forced to give the far from athletic Carr an unbroken spell of one and a half hours at the bowling crease, a decision which added to the fury of the press. To cap it all, with Bardsley's score at 70, a simple chance went into and out of MacLaren's anguished hands at slip. It was immediately forgotten that the same player had survived a far more vital catch to England's wicket-keeper Lilley (recently made a grandfather) with his score a mere 19; it was necessary to look no further than MacLaren for the cause of England's blundering.

After such a day of misfortune one can but admire the brave decision he made in electing to open the England innings himself with just forty-five minutes left to play. Sadly, the only partnership MacLaren and Spooner made for England was short-lived, both being dismissed before close of play. Cotter was able to make the ball fly alarmingly and his great pace proved too much for Archie who was lbw to a full toss for only 12 in his last Test match innings. The match finished a rather tame draw, as it would probably have done whatever team had been selected for England, but the rumblings of discontent continued: 'There was an angry feeling that our downfall was courted by mismanagement,' said Wisden. 'The selectors made the worst possible use of the material available,' echoed P. F. Warner.

Certainly, bad selections had not helped England's cause but the plain fact was that the batting had let the side down. This is hardly surprising when one considers the great Golden Age players who were unavailable—Jackson, Ranji, Foster—those that were injured—Jessop, Hobbs, Hayward—plus the indifferent form of Fry and MacLaren. Place these facts alongside five lost tosses and the absence of Blythe after he had taken eighteen wickets in two games and defeat was not really surprising. MacLaren's personal reputation as a leader and Test match player was irreparably harmed; like an ageing boxer he had stayed on for just one fight too many.

With MacLaren's Test match career ended it was widely assumed that he would be making very few appearances for Lancashire in the future. It was surprising, therefore, when the 1910 season began with MacLaren a regular member of a highly successful county team. After the tribulations of the previous summer perhaps Archie felt he had something to prove—to himself as well as to the public. He had scored only two first-class centuries in the five seasons since the championship-winning year of 1904, and his most recent form for Lancashire in 1909 had been very poor.

This lack of success continued in Lancashire's early games during May 1910, but then in the first week of June everything seemed to come right with two vintage centuries in the space of three days. The first, against Warwickshire at Edgbaston, was as brilliant an innings as any in his entire career. The grumblings about MacLaren's presence in the team at the expense of younger players had been gaining in strength but this display silenced all criticism. Archie, batting at number six, was 1 not out when the final day's play began with Lancashire needing quick runs for a declaration. In ninety glorious minutes 126 runs were added and MacLaren's personal score stood on 94 as Frank Field ran in to bowl at him. That imperious front foot was once more planted down the wicket, and from the most famous of high backlifts the ball was sent crashing back high over the bowler's head and into the pavilion for six. Hornby immediately signalled the declaration but it understandably took some time to persuade MacLaren away from the wicket—he claimed that he thought the captain was offering him a drink!

Archie was really in the mood now and the next game, at Worcester, saw another meteoric innings 'in his incomparable style of eight or ten years ago', according to a contemporary account. The Lancashire innings was tottering at 180 for five when MacLaren was joined by Ralph Whitehead, who two years earlier had achieved the double of scoring a century and being no-balled for throwing on his first-class debut. On this occasion the pair set about the Worcestershire bowling to such effect that 260 runs were added in only two and a half hours, MacLaren's share being a magnificent 127. Archie was revitalised and to show that he had energy to spare he finished the drawn game by bowling two overs of assorted lobs which cost 25 runs.

MacLaren had proved his point and now, unpredictable as ever, he called a halt just when even his sternest critics were clamouring for more. He was to play the occasional game in the future, and even to go on overseas tours, but as far as regular cricket for Lancashire was concerned this was the end. He had begun on a high note twenty years earlier and now he wanted to finish on one.

Although it was said that MacLaren had lost his appetite for cricket this was purely temporary. In February and March of 1912 the MCC sent a team to Argentina under the captaincy of Lord Hawke, and Archie was included at his own request. This was the first tour to South America from anywhere outside that continent and the all-amateur team was a strong one, containing six Test players. The full side was: H. H. C. Baird, M. C. Bird, C. E. de Trafford, W. Findlay, E. J. Fulcher, C. E. Hatfield, Lord Hawke, A. J. L. Hill, A. C. MacLaren, L. H. W. Troughton, N. C. Tufnell, and E. R. Wilson (J. O. Anderson also played in an emergency).

The tourists may have been a little surprised at the standard of play in Argentina, for they drew the first two games and then lost to a representative Argentinian team. Subsequently they buckled down to it, winning the other six matches including the two remaining unofficial 'Tests'. MacLaren had rather a mixed time, starting the tour with scores of 0, 0, 0, 0 and 7. Since his last two innings, in club matches in England, had also been scoreless he could well be described as experiencing a bad patch. Archie's form returned, with a score of 172 against a side of Argentinian-born players, N. C. Tufnell helping him add 314 for the third wicket. MacLaren also took a turn at captaining the side when Lord Hawke suffered a leg injury. The tour was an interesting one from a cricket point of view and, judging from Lord Hawke's book of reminiscences, was also thoroughly enjoyable.

Over the next couple of years Archie was clearly restless at not playing any serious cricket. At about this time he teamed up with Lionel Robinson, a strange character whom we shall meet again in the following chapter. Archie began playing in Robinson's high-standard country house cricket and in February 1914, when the desire to play again became overwhelming, he wrote to the Lancashire club offering his services.

It was also in 1914 that Archie entered into another of his optimistic business schemes, this time the publication of a cricket magazine entitled *The World of Cricket*. This was intended as a successor to *Cricket. A Weekly Record of the Game* which, although it had run continuously for thirty-two years, had recently experienced a serious decline in circulation. The paper had been acquired in 1911 by J. N. Pentelow, a cricket historian and statistician, who now formed a partnership with MacLaren in an effort to boost sales. MacLaren was described as editor, with Pentelow as his assistant, but the latter apparently performed most of the production duties. Pentelow was no great businessman but the acquisition of MacLaren as partner was the final recipe for complete disaster, and by the end of the year the business had collapsed. Pentelow was apparently left to take care of all the financial debts and the worry appeared to age him almost overnight. Although only forty years old his hair turned white, his shoulders became bowed and his face lined. Apart from cricket Pentelow also wrote stories for boys' magazines and in order to pay off his debts he had to spend day and night producing as much as possible. He was quoted as saying of the financial collapse, 'It cost me some hundreds of pounds – which sounds extravagant. But I ran it at a heavy loss, and MacLaren let me down so badly that the loss was doubled.' Although the details are somewhat obscure, it appears that MacLaren's characteristic unreliability with money left Pentelow very much in the lurch.

Throughout the cricket season Archie managed to play several first-class and club games in order to get into some sort of form. Perhaps he hoped to bolster the popularity of *The World of Cricket* by his appearances, and he certainly mentioned several times in the paper that he was planning a return to the Lancashire side. Strangely, considering his letter to the club in February, he made a great point of emphasising that his imminent return was due to pressure from his friends and at the request of the county. In the event his one county appearance was against Surrey at the Oval where he scored only 4 and 0 in a heavy defeat. War was about to be declared and MacLaren strongly opposed the continuation of professional cricket. As the season came to a premature close, not to be re-opened for another five years, it seemed that Archie's farewell appearance on a first-class cricket field had seen him clean bowled by Bill Hitch for nought.

10

A Parting Shot—
Eastbourne

In October 1914 Archie enlisted as a Lieutenant in the Royal
Army Service Corps and immediately embarked on a recruiting
campaign with Captain G. L. Jessop. By October 1917 MacLaren
too had risen to the rank of Captain but was then invalided out of
the service having spent three years in the recruiting service in and
around Manchester. Although county cricket began again in 1919
MacLaren, now aged 47, had neither the fitness nor the time to
take part, unlike his old friends Spooner and Fry who briefly
revived memories of the Golden Age. By 1921, though, when
Warwick Armstrong brought over the first official post-war touring side (an Australian Forces team containing the nucleus of
Armstrong's XI had played here in 1919), Archie was back in the
forefront although not playing any county cricket himself. He was
writing in the newspapers as well as the newly established *Cricketer*
magazine and could always be relied on to give his views on the
present generation of cricketers, in particular the Australians.
Archie was also acting at this time as cricket manager for Lionel
Robinson who owned a 2,000-acre estate in the village of Old
Buckenham near Attleborough, fifteen miles south-west of
Norwich. MacLaren and his wife and children lived in a cottage on
the estate for several years at a time when finances were at rock
bottom.

Robinson was born in Ceylon but brought up in Melbourne where he became a hugely prosperous stockbroker, and through his keen interest in cricket and horse racing doubtless met up with MacLaren's in-laws. In the early years of the century his financial interests brought him to London where he became a powerful figure in the city, but it was as an English-style landed gentleman that he really sought recognition. To this end he bought and extravagantly rebuilt his estate in Norfolk, erected splendid stables for a racing stud, organised extensive shooting facilities and laid out his own private cricket ground. No expense was spared to prepare a hard, fast Australian-style wicket even to the extent of importing special turf from the Antipodes. Archie was the ideal man to help organise and participate in the country house matches that Robinson thought would help gain him acceptance into the aristocracy. Unfortunately he never quite made it—even his enormous wealth could not disguise his obstinate, aggressive nature and propensity for abusive slanging matches. However, with the cricket, the racehorse breeding and the lavish hospitality, it was a natural setting for Archie who must often have reflected how well he could have carried it off if only he had been blessed with Robinson's financial resources. It must have been strangely ironic to hear the aristocratically spoken, yet penniless, Archie advising his ostentatious millionaire employer.

It was in this season of 1921 that MacLaren pulled off the greatest coup for Robinson's ambitions as a patron of cricket. The mighty Australians played the second match of their tour at Old Buckenham against a team selected and captained by Archie but labelled Lionel Robinson's XI. The team was a strong one and reflected Archie's feelings on the merits of certain players with a particular accent on amateur talent. There was the experience of the current England captain, J. W. H. T. Douglas, D. J. Knight, Vallance Jupp, P. G. H. Fender and J. C. White, plus the invaluable services of the two leading professional batsmen, Hobbs and Hendren. The team was completed by MacLaren himself and a contingent of three prominent Cambridge University players— G. E. C. Wood, C. H. Gibson and A. P. F. Chapman. These last two were still undergraduates and their obvious talents had greatly impressed Archie who played a large part in the encouragement of their early development. The team had been selected with the idea of fast scoring, accurate bowling and, most important, brilliant fielding.

On the appointed day 2,000 spectators poured into the picturesque ground from all over East Anglia, many being fetched the four miles from the railway station by a non-stop pony and trap convoy. Their excitement was dulled, though, by heavy rain and even snow, which limited their first glimpse of the Australians to the pre-match practice and less than fifteen minutes actual play. Next day the skies were brighter and a crowd estimated at between seven and ten thousand saw the Australians shot out for a paltry 136 which was to remain their lowest total for the entire tour. The wicket, whilst not easy, was never vicious and the away-swing of Douglas (six for 64) and the accuracy of Gibson (three for 33) polished off the opposition by mid-afternoon. When Robinson's XI batted on this quick wicket the effects of the rain made the speed and breakback of Ted McDonald even more devastating than usual. Soon Knight was dismissed but Hobbs and Jupp settled in to bat as well as anyone would all summer against the twin threat of McDonald and Gregory. Finally both were forced to retire hurt, Jupp with a broken finger and Hobbs with a badly torn thigh muscle, his 85 being the only innings he would play against the tourists all that season. But for these two McDonald would surely have ripped through the rest of the batting, and Hobbs later called this classic confrontation the finest innings of his career considering the conditions.

On the last day the scratch XI moved from 156 for one to 256 for nine declared but rain ruined any hope of a finish with the Australians on 25 for one. One of the happiest features of an otherwise grey day was a brief innings of 25 not out by Archie who batted number eleven and drove the fast bowlers for five rousing boundaries before declaring. After this the Australian openers were far from happy before the rain came, Clem Gibson maintaining his reputation for accuracy with an analysis of $9-8-1-1$.

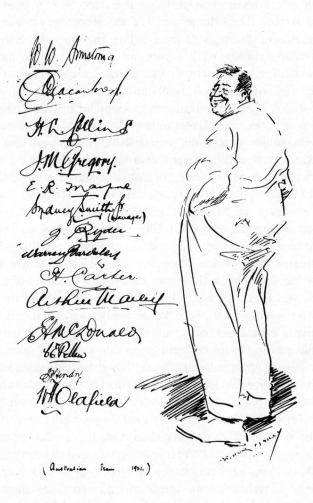

A cartoon of Warwick Armstrong drawn by Arthur Mailey with the accompanying signatures of the 1921 Australians. MacLaren's son, Ian, collected this marvellous page for his scrapbook at the Attleborough match in which his father was captain.

131

As the Australians went on to humiliate a dispirited England in the Test series most people forgot this match at Attleborough, but not Archie. The summer of 1921 was blisteringly hot and suited the Australian attack of fast bowling and leg spin perfectly, but MacLaren considered they were flattered by the results and that he had detected a few faults on those two cold days in early May. Throughout the season the man who was so often branded a pessimist took every opportunity to speak up for English prospects, as long as the correct players were chosen. He pressed the claims of the younger generation, especially Clem Gibson and Hubert Ashton, but such calls were ignored by the selectors.

Sadly, only two members of that all-conquering Australian side are still alive, H. L. Hendry and C. E. Pellew. Hendry, now eighty-five years of age, has kindly contributed the following memories of Archie from that season of 1921: 'Our team in England saw a lot of Archie; whenever we returned to London, he and his pal Walter Brearley always came along to the Cecil Hotel, where we were staying, for a chat with Warwick and other members of our team, and was ever anxious to know what we thought of the county players we met on the tour. We honestly told them the truth about players' capabilities but as time went on, Archie suspected we were endeavouring to get certain players into your Test team, particularly after Dipper failed in a Test although he had made a lot of runs against us for Gloucestershire. We had great fun with these two who were old friends of Warwick. Archie was a great judge of cricket and cricketers, and had a keen sense of humour. After our tour of Scotland where Kerr, their captain, was allowed to score a century, Archie said, ''You have overstepped the mark this time, fellows. You have no chance of getting us to pick Kerr in the Tests!'' Archie was also astute enough to realise something was going on at Manchester when the Hon. Lionel Tennyson tried to close his innings contrary to your own rules. After rain ruined the first day's play, it made it compulsory to close before ten to five; we had the rule book opened in our dressing room before taking the field after the adjournment. We kept watching the clock and were relieved when the time for closure had expired. Archie told us afterwards that watching with the selectors he said, ''There is something important going on, those Australians are constantly looking at the clock.''!'

Archie was following the progress of the Australians with all the intensity he had shown when he was captain of England, but his interest was far from purely academic. Much to his delight the Eastbourne Cricket Club invited him to select and captain 'An England XI' to play the tourists at the Saffrons in a match after the final Test. As the game approached and England's fortunes waned, Archie staunchly maintained that he would beat Armstrong's invincibles. MacLaren's critics, of which there were always plenty, awaited the outcome with a certain smugness for up until the Eastbourne game the Australian record was played 36, won 22, lost 0. Amongst others S. H. Pardon, who had been so critical in 1909, pointed out that Archie's own record for Test match selections had never been very successful and that anybody could criticise from the sidelines.

To help in his team selection Archie went up to Cambridge at the beginning of June to watch the Australians beat the University by an innings and 14 runs. In spite of this drubbing MacLaren's keen cricketing perception saw enough promise to invite six of the University team to join his side. These were the three brothers, Gilbert, Hubert and Claude Ashton, C. S. Marriott, Percy Chapman and Gibson. As the game approached he also recruited the experience of Aubrey Faulkner, the old South African all-rounder now aged thirty-eight, who was coaching in England, G. N. Foster, one of the famous brotherhood, and Michael Falcon who, despite only playing for Norfolk, had been one of Archie's proposed choices for the Tests. The wicket-keeper was to be George Wood who had played at Attleborough. In the event Marriott was ill and his place was taken by MacLaren's old team-mate and crony, Walter Brearley. George Wood had kept wicket to the 47-year-old fast bowler earlier in the 1921 season and was able to confirm Brearley's own opinion that the ball thudded into the gloves with all its old force. Seven or eight years later when Gerald Hough played with Brearley in Cheshire, he was told, 'If I were to play for

Somerset now, they would win the championship.' He certainly never lacked confidence.

The preparations for this match provided MacLaren with just the situation he revelled in—complete authority to select a side which could carry out his tactical theories. His plans were evolved with minute attention to detail. Knowing that this would almost certainly be his last tilt at the Australians he was determined to go out in style.

What then were his tactics? Archie had no delusions that the Australians were anything other than an outstanding side, although he thought them inferior to the great Joe Darling team with the very notable exception of McDonald. He considered that England's defeat was due to sub-standard bowling which failed to take advantage of a tendency that Archie had noticed for the Australians to play across the line of the ball on the back foot. Unerring accuracy and a degree of spin were required, hence the choice of Falcon, Gibson, Marriott and Faulkner, all noted for their steadiness. The other factor which he had repeatedly criticised was the slack fielding of the England teams and it was for this reason, as much as their batting, that the three Ashtons and Chapman were selected. Perhaps most important of all, Archie wanted to have a go at Australia with a completely amateur team. He was a great admirer of many professionals but he looked back on the great days of amateur batsmen with nostalgia, always preaching that the modern player lacked the attacking spirit of the Golden Age.

The hand-picked team finally arrived at Eastbourne and, although not one of the thirty players who had represented England that season was included, Archie was confident enough to invite Neville Cardus along to report the match with the intriguing 'I think I know how to beat Armstrong's lot'. There were 9,000 people at the ground for the first day's play, many of them on holiday. The England XI won the toss and Archie had no hesitation in batting first on the usual perfect Saffrons wicket in hot sunny weather. It was then that catastrophe struck. Jack Gregory injured his thumb almost immediately and had to withdraw but his illustrious partner, Ted McDonald, brushed aside the English batting with deadly precision. Armstrong's gently rolled leg spinners shared the wickets and, after seventy-five minutes of gentle exercise for the Australians, MacLaren's team were all out for a pitiful 43. The over-riding feeling amongst the spectators who had come for one last glimpse of MacLaren was one of embarrassment—he was, despite all his talk, just a has-been. The batting was later described by Gilbert Ashton as 'deplorably weak' and contemporary reports speak of wickets being recklessly thrown away by careless shots. Only Chapman, with 16, reached double figures and the total of 43 was the lowest ever in a first-class match at Eastbourne. To cap it all, Walter Brearley, one of only four bowlers in the side, pulled a leg muscle whilst batting and took no further part in the game except to be run out for 0 in the second innings with a runner.

Was MacLaren a dejected pessimist at lunchtime? Surprisingly not, according to a letter to the author from Gilbert Ashton, who was struck by his calmness throughout the game—'the only person who appeared to be completely unmoved by this disastrous start was MacLaren'. But the task of containing the Australians on a perfect wicket appeared to be impossible when after ninety minutes the score was 80 for one, with Falcon and Gibson looking very ordinary. At this point Archie replaced Gibson with Faulkner who, finding some turn for his leg breaks and googlies, immediately bowled Macartney and Andrews. The rest of the team responded magnificently, Falcon found his length and the youngsters fielded like tigers to restrict the score to 174, a lead of 131. With a few minutes left in which to take a vital wicket or two, Armstrong's men must have had their sights on a victory within two days.

MacLaren now employed one of his favourite tactics of former days—a change in the batting order to suit the situation. It was essential that he protect his attacking batsmen until the next day so George Wood, number eight in the first innings, was promoted. Who else could be considered dispensable enough to bear the brunt of McDonald and Gregory in fading light? A buzz of expectation ran through the crowd as they saw the white-haired veteran, MacLaren, turning the clock back twenty years as he strode out

135

once again to open the innings. This could hardly have been an easy decision. If he had batted late the next day with the game as good as over he might have found the Australians in relatively generous mood for what would probably be his last first-class innings.

Bravely Archie weathered the storm that evening but next morning he played back to the first ball from McDonald and was clean bowled. The next batsman was Gilbert Ashton and for the first time the fight was carried to the Australians. He lasted only half an hour but the way was pointed for his brother Hubert and the veteran Aubrey Faulkner to launch their historic partnership. Coming together at 60 for four the pair put on 154 in three and a half hours before Ashton was trapped for 75. At first they played themselves in very carefully but gradually they opened out until the bowling was really collared. After Ashton left Faulkner went on and on to reach a magnificent 153, while McDonald finished with a well earned six for 98. With 196 needed for victory the Australians lost Collins in the forty-five minutes play of that second evening.

On the last morning Archie had his side keyed up for a final do or die effort. Gibson and Falcon bowled as if their lives depended on it and the Australians were fighting for every run against the eager young fielders. By lunch the score was 106 for five, three wickets to Gibson, two to Falcon and brilliant slip catches by Hubert and Claude Ashton. News of the score quickly spread and a large crowd began to form for the afternoon's play. Gilbert Ashton, who was doubtless feeling the tension himself, was again struck by MacLaren's bearing: 'Only MacLaren remained as calm and unmoved as at lunch on that first day.' The late Sir Hubert Ashton remembered his slipcatch during that morning's play as follows: 'At a very critical point in the Australian second innings, Archie was fielding second slip and I first. Pellew mishit a ball from Clem Gibson and sent up a semi-skier – it was clearly his catch rather than mine but we looked at each other. He said quietly, "I think you may have that one," folded his arms and turned away. Thank Heaven I held it to be rewarded by, "Well done – but I never had any doubt."'

After the break Andrews and Ryder started to attack and had taken the score to 140 for five when the tired Falcon was replaced by the spin of Faulkner. This was the crucial move of the game. Seeing the chance to finish things quickly Jack Ryder slashed wildly at Gibson and was caught in the covers by the third Ashton brother, Gilbert. This was the only wicket in the whole innings which fell to a rash shot. Two balls later Jack Gregory was leg before to Gibson at 143 for seven. The accurate spin of Faulkner, coupled with brilliant fielding, now trapped the Australians in a web from which there was no respite. Andrews groped forward to a teasing delivery on his leg stump, the ball pitched, lifted and neatly removed the off bail. This brought in the giant, apparently impassive, Armstrong who had first played against MacLaren in Tests twenty years previously. He was the last hope of preserving the Australians' unbeaten record and he was not going to give his wicket away foolishly. The 'Big Ship', as he was known, had never been the most mobile of batsmen against slow bowlers and now he looked distinctly unhappy facing Faulkner. He stabbed defensively without moving his feet, but the loud appeal which followed the impact of ball on pad was disallowed. The next delivery from the experienced South African was identical. Again the nervous prod failed to make contact and this time the umpire's finger was raised in answer to the frantic appeal. The score was 154 for nine.

This was the finish and although the last pair edged the score to within 29 of the required total, it was merely a question of time before Gibson slipped one through Mailey's defence and the game was over. The impossible had happened and a weary MacLaren led his team from the field surrounded by an enthusiastic throng of onrushing spectators. Gilbert Ashton summed it up: 'My abiding memory of the game will always be of the imperturbability of MacLaren. He had given the side hope when all seemed lost, courage and inspiration. At the end, calm and dignified, he led his side off the field.'

In many ways this game, although not vitally important to a tired Australian team, was one of the greatest triumphs of Archie's career. It was ironic that in his heyday, at the height of his powers, things had always seemed to go wrong at the vital moment, yet now in his last big game the fates had relented. After all the ups and downs of the last thirty years, including an unfair amount of criticism, Archie must have felt immensely satisfied. He had justified everything he had been saying all season, particularly his pleas for the inclusion of Gibson, Falcon and Hubert Ashton.

Weary though the Australians were, there is no evidence that they treated the game light-heartedly. It was important to them that they go through the season undefeated and they played their full Test team with the exception of Taylor, for whom Jack Ryder was a more than capable replacement. H. L. Hendry has, however, written to the author as follows: 'Although not playing at Eastbourne, I was present, and always felt Warwick Armstrong lost the match for us by taking too much for granted and putting himself in nearly last in the second innings.' It seems that, on this occasion at least, MacLaren had outwitted the Australian captain.

On a more humorous note Archie went up to his old friend Walter Brearley after the game and thanked him warmly for contributing to the victory. An amazed Brearley reminded him that he had hardly taken part at all and had not bowled a single ball. Back came the reply, 'Exactly, Walter, that's why we won.' This may seem cruel but these two old contemporaries always enjoyed a joke at each other's expense. Cardus tells a famous story of seeing the pair in a train compartment and overhearing their conversation which consisted of, 'You're a bloody fine slip fielder!' and 'You're a bloody fine fast bowler!' Stories of Brearley are legion and an account of his turbulent career would fill a book. Indeed, when the Old Trafford pavilion attendant, William Howard, told MacLaren that he was going to write his reminiscences, Archie was so concerned at what he might reveal that he suggested the whole book be devoted to tales about Brearley. MacLaren and Brearley were very much partners in crime both on the field and off it. At one time they were both representatives for a particular brand of whisky but, as usual, with little success.

The late Sir Hubert Ashton vividly recalled the evening of the Eastbourne victory as follows:

STATION-BLANKNEY.
TELEGRAPH-METHERINGHAM.
TELEPHONE-8 METHERINGHAM.

MANOR HOUSE.

METHERINGHAM,

LINCOLN.

Aug: 31: 21

Dear Old Tavish

So pleased to see that you won such a splendid match against the Australians and send my very best congratulations I hope you are not knocked up at all although I expect a strenuous game doesn't do you much good now a days. I see in your reported speech that you don't intend playing any more and if this is really true I sh? just like to say how pleased I am that you have finished up so splendidly. The best of luck yours

Reggie Spooner

Dont bother to answer this.

After the Eastbourne match countless letters and telegrams of congratulation arrived for Archie. This one from his old comrade, Reggie Spooner, is typical of the sentiment.

My father was a devoted Lancastrian and a great admirer of Archie MacLaren. On the night of our victory we were all staying at the same hotel and my two brothers and I together with our father and mother were coming towards the end of dinner when we were joined by Archie and Walter Brearley. Now these two gentlemen had been celebrating – as they were fully entitled to do – and I was a little nervous as to what might transpire, as my mother was rather against strong language. They sat down for the best part of an hour and were extremely amusing, each contradicting the other in their reminiscences and saying they were 'bloody liars'. However they never offended in any way and it is one of the happiest recollections of my life to recall the tears of pleasure falling from the eyes of our parents. Those two famous Lancastrians were a wonderful knockabout turn.

In September 1921, shortly after the Eastbourne success, the Lancashire club offered MacLaren an appointment as coach for the following season. Archie's finances had not improved since the war so the £550 salary for one summer's work was a godsend, certainly enough to overcome his aversion to being regarded as a mere employee. The announcement was roundly applauded by the press and county supporters alike who saw MacLaren as the ideal man to bring on the younger players. The committee presented Archie with a ten-point curriculum outlining his duties, which included captaining the second XI, organising schoolboy nets in the Easter holidays and general day to day coaching. The last point in the list struck a warning note: 'It is understood that any articles you desire to write for the press must in no way interfere with your duties, and under no circumstances must they allude to Lancashire cricket.' A distinct change in atmosphere from the easy-going days when Archie was captain of the county side.

The appointment did not begin until April 1922 but, true to form, Archie had already received a £300 advance on his salary before 1921 was out. In January the Lancashire committee received a further application for £50 which was granted with the proviso that no more advances would be paid at least until MacLaren had started work!

One of the young second XI players who was coached by

MacLaren was Len Hopwood, later to represent England against Australia. In those days Hopwood was just another young hopeful, but he was so influenced by Archie that he would wait near his lodgings in order to meet the great man 'accidentally' and walk to the grounds with him. Some years ago Hopwood chronicled his reminiscences of that season for the *Manchester Evening News* and they are now reproduced with his kind permission.

A great influence in my youth was A. C. MacLaren, one of those who dominated the cricket scene in such majestic fashion in the early days of the present century which so many eminent authorities have described as the Golden Age. I came under the spell of MacLaren when he was coach at Old Trafford.

Autocrat, undoubtedly, he was. His word was law. Yet he was kind in his autocracy and almost fanatical in his regard for the young player's well-being. Typical of this was his reply to a request from my own local club that I should be granted leave of absence from Old Trafford on Saturdays to play for my own local club and so gain league experience. 'I will be pleased to let him off when I can. I am, however, nervous about youngsters being overworked. They want as much nursing as two-year-old colts. The boy has good promise and I have great hopes of him playing for the county later. I don't want him overworked,' he wrote.

In similar vein but with more pungent comment was his reply to a personal request. In Club and Ground matches I seemed to be a permanent number ten in the batting order. I hinted to him that the runs I was scoring there entitled me to promotion. Those hopes were dashed immediately. 'So you want to be an all-rounder. Let me tell you this, my boy. To be an all-rounder a man must be as strong as an ox or a fool. You are neither. As long as I am at Old Trafford you will be number ten.' And that was that.

MacLaren was incredible in the manner in which he got his own way. My first appearance in the Lancashire second XI was a typical example of his determination – one might even say cunning.

The morning after my selection in the team to play Cheshire at Heywood had been announced in the Manchester evening papers secretary Harry Rylance casually informed me that I had not been picked. My name had got in the list by mistake! I would not go to Heywood.

141

I was broken-hearted. MacLaren realised this but he said nothing. He preferred to act. A couple of days later I received an imperious command to present myself at the nets. Waiting for me was MacLaren, padded up and bat in hand. Behind him was an array of committee men. For the next quarter of an hour I bowled my heart out at the great man. I didn't know what was afoot but I had a feeling it was a vital moment in my career. And so it proved to be.

At the end of it MacLaren and the committee went into a huddle. I was informed that I would go to Heywood as twelfth man. This news created terrific astonishment in the Dog's Home, as the professionals' dressing room was then called. Never before had a Lancashire second team boasted a twelfth man.

I arrived at Heywood prepared to be the errand boy. Instead I found myself in the middle. MacLaren, who normally skippered the side, couldn't play. He was afflicted with a sudden attack of lumbago!

On rare occasions he would descend from his Olympian heights and fascinate we youngsters with his stories of cricket and cricketers. We revelled in his accounts of cut and thrust with W. G. Grace.

One that appealed to me was his description of the toss when Lancashire played Gloucestershire at the Liverpool club's lovely ground at Aigburth. The wicket was a beauty. This was a toss to win.

MacLaren asked Grace to call, then tossed the coin high and far. With almost indecent haste he followed the coin in its flight, bent down, picked it up and triumphantly announced, 'Bad luck W.G., we'll bat.' W.G. protested vociferously. 'I never saw it,' he exploded. 'Nor did I at Cheltenham,' retorted MacLaren.

My abiding impression of MacLaren as a coach is that he made one think for oneself. Though never unorthodox—a batsman of such classic style as he could never be that—he nevertheless disdained the generally accepted coaching methods of 'left elbow well forward' and the like.

One doesn't remember him talking or demonstrating a lot, in the nets, that is. He didn't coach cricket into one. By some mysterious means he drew one's talents out then developed them. Sometimes he coaxed, at other times he bullied. I have vivid memories of one of his bullying techniques. He took me to the nets, stood in the umpire's position at the bowling end and commanded me to spin the ball. I suppose I had at that time what used to be called the left hander's natural spin. That, indeed, was all I knew about spin.

I bowled and bowled. More insistent became the demands to 'spin it'.

Finally, and in a thunderous tone, he roared 'Spin the bloody ball!' It was the first time I had heard him swear. I was galvanised into action. The next ball turned. I had spun it! So did the next, and the next. MacLaren walked away, satisfied. I was too.

Here was an example of MacLaren's technique. He didn't try to teach one to spin the ball as other's spun it. He made one think for one's self and arrive at an individual solution by a process of trial and error.

Another of MacLaren's young charges was Malcolm Taylor who later played many games for the county before becoming a leading coach. Sadly, Taylor died in 1978 but in his closing days he wrote of MacLaren in glowing terms: 'As a boy of 17, it was the first time I had ever met a real *Gentleman*. We boys thought him a most kind man, and as a coach he was a wonderful man. He taught me that no batsman worth his salt would allow bowlers such as Lol Larwood, Bill Voce or Frank Matthews to bowl at him without a long-off or long-on.'

Hopwood and Taylor played throughout the season with MacLaren and both developed tremendous respect and affection for him. Not everybody at Old Trafford shared this view of course, and at first meeting he could be a trifle brusque especially if the weather was damp and his rheumatism troublesome. A youngster named John Wild attended a trial that year, 1922, along with other hopeful boys and confessed that Archie 'scared the pants off us'.

Perhaps the most memorable occasion for the young players that season was a Club and Ground match in which Reggie Spooner made a rare appearance. Archie, who invariably batted number eleven, decided that he and Reggie could indulge themselves this once and they duly took the opportunity to open together for the last time. Sadly, they only scored a handful of runs between them but young Len Hopwood's attention was caught by a pull shot from MacLaren, the like of which he had never seen before or since. When he returned to the pavilion Archie appeared most satisfied with the brief innings, saying, 'Well, I am glad I can still play that shot.'

Despite MacLaren's undoubted ability as a coach all was not well at Old Trafford. His autocratic manner did not impress the committee and they resented being told what to do by the second XI coach. To make matters worse, Archie knew more about cricket than any of those who were making the decisions. William Howard's, book of reminiscences contains several tales of MacLaren's independent attitude and distaste for regular hours or routine. As in his playing career and business ventures he was incapable of working with or for other people. He required the position of dictator. Never one to hide his opinions, Archie even compiled a blacklist of members and committee men who disapproved of him and with whom he had argued. It was Howard's job to look out for anyone on the list and steer them well clear of Archie. There was no such ill feeling where the players were concerned. Although he was a strict disciplinarian he could be an endearing companion off the field, and the young players responded just as they had at Eastbourne. J. S. Cragg, a former player and more recently President of Lancashire, writes, 'I found him to be a very friendly and easy-going character, and nothing of the ''great I am'' about him.'

Despite the friction there were many benefits from MacLaren's season as coach. Apart from his beneficial influence over the players, he also proposed the revolutionary step of building an indoor practice area. Unfortunately the committee were not keen on listening to the idea, which would have cost £840, and the project was shelved until 1951. In this instance Archie was ahead of his time but in many ways his way of life was now out of place. His distinguished, upright figure in brightly coloured blazer was an unhappy reminder that the Golden Age had passed for ever. Archie's active cricket career was also almost over, even though there was to be one more triumph before he finally accepted a back seat.

11
Swan Song

The MCC arranged to send out two touring teams during the winter of 1922–3, one to South Africa and the other to Australia and New Zealand. The former was to be the senior tour with a full series of five Test matches, whereas the latter was envisaged as more of a goodwill visit and as a means of giving experience to some of England's more promising young amateur cricketers. The fourteen-match tour of New Zealand, including three representative games, was to be sandwiched between two groups of matches against the Australian state teams. The tour was an important stepping stone towards the granting of full Test match status to New Zealand in 1929. During the nineteenth century, six of the privately organised teams sent to Australia had also stopped off for the odd game in New Zealand, and since then more extensive visits had been made by Lord Hawke's XI in 1902–3 and by an amateur MCC side in 1906–7. The home teams had shown a gradual improvement in standard, culminating in victory in one of the representative games on this last tour. By 1922 another visit was long overdue.

Since the team was to be comprised mainly of young amateurs the choice of MacLaren as captain was a sensible and a popular one. Not only did Archie have more experience of Australian conditions than any other Englishman, but his recent triumph with a team of amateur cricketers at Eastbourne had indicated his ability to get the best out of youngsters. He was the ideal man to encourage

145

and improve talented but inexperienced players. Perhaps the image Archie had with the public at this time is best shown by a poem written by D. L. A. Jephson shortly before the team left England.

> Good luck to the skipper who sails today –
> The veteran skilled and wise,
> Who knows the game from the first great A
> To the Z at the tail that lies;
> A leader born and a judge of men,
> Still able to play his part –
> A tower of strength to the other ten,
> With the fire of his dauntless heart.

Although a little dated in style, several of these phrases accurately sum up just why Archie was chosen for the job.

The team Archie was to lead consisted of the following players:

A. C. MacLaren (Lancs)

C. H. Gibson (Camb. U., Sussex)

A. P. F. Chapman (Camb. U.)

J. C. Hartley (Oxford U., Sussex)

T. C. Lowry (Camb. U., Som.)

A. P. Freeman (Kent)

C. H. Titchmarsh (Herts)

H. Tyldesley (Lancs)

G. Wilson (Camb. U., Yorks.)

Hon. F. S. G. Calthorpe (Camb. U., Warwicks.)

W. A. C. Wilkinson (Oxf. U., Army)

Hon. D. F. Brand (Camb. U.)

J. F. MacLean (Worcs.)

W. W. Hill-Wood (Camb. U., Derbys.)

B. S. Hill-Wood also assisted in several games.

Of these only twelve appeared in first-class cricket during 1922, four of them being members of the Cambridge University side. For this reason the Australian and New Zealand public regarded the team as being of very poor quality and they were even described as 'picnic tourists'. In fact, in 1922 the standard of cricket outside the county championship was much higher than it is today and some of these lesser-known players were highly talented. The young brigade was represented by Chapman, Lowry, Wilson, Gibson, Brand and W. W. Hill-Wood. Percy Chapman, aged twenty-two, who had played for MacLaren at Eastbourne and Attleborough, was regarded by most judges of the game, including Archie, as the most promising English cricketer for years. A dashing left-handed batsman and electric fielder, he had already dominated the 1922 Gentlemen v. Players match at Lord's and was unlucky to miss the South African tour. He had not yet qualified for Kent and during the University vacations was playing for his native Berkshire. Just as the MCC's chief batting hopes rested with Chapman so the bowling would rely heavily on his former Cambridge team mate, Clem Gibson. Another Eastbourne veteran, Gibson (also aged 22) had been temporarily lost to English cricket after that famous match when he returned to Argentina. No doubt at the instigation of MacLaren, he took time off from the family business to join this tour. His bowling success stemmed from an impeccable length, variation of pace and a peculiar flight, all produced by a perfect quick bowler's action.

Of the rest Wilson had met with great success at Harrow before the war and had just captained Yorkshire to the 1922 county championship. T. C. Lowry was to become one of New Zealand's finest batsmen and the Hon. D. F. Brand was a late replacement for R. St L. Fowler of Fowler's match fame. Fowler, an experienced player, could not get leave from the Army and Brand was chosen, on Lord Harris' recommendation, after captaining Eton in 1921.

Amongst the more experienced players much reliance was to be placed on the batting of W. A. C. Wilkinson and C. H. Titchmarsh and the all-round ability of F. S. G. Calthorpe, who had come close to doing the double for Warwickshire in 1922. To this collection of public school and university products were added two professional leg-break and googly bowlers in 'Tich' Freeman and Harry Tyldesley. Archie's experience of Australian conditions was responsible for their inclusion; he remembered especially the use he had made of Len Braund in 1901-2. Of the two, Freeman had just started the tremendous run of success he was to have in county cricket with a stack of wickets in 1922, but Harry Tyldesley was virtually unknown having played only four games for Lancashire and taken four wickets. Archie had seen plenty of him in the second XI and was hopeful that he would prove to be another 'MacLaren special'.

Although the team appeared to most Australians and New Zealanders to be a motley collection of amateurs intent on a pleasant cricketing holiday, it was far from that. MacLaren himself had never seen half the team play before but, although he thought that the leading Australian state sides would be too strong for them, he was confident that the New Zealanders would be beaten. In fact he announced his intention of playing without the two professional bowlers whenever the standard of the opposition allowed. On a personal note he added, 'I shall be disappointed if I do not get a few runs if I keep fit. I have not lost all my confidence by a long way.' This last sentence would certainly have amused anybody who knew Archie personally.

The following description of the tour is built around the reminiscences of Alex Wilkinson who was a leading member of the MCC team. Col Wilkinson has kindly written his account especially for this biography of Archie MacLaren and in it he provides much fascinating detail of this little known tour. At intervals the narrative has been supplemented by some additional facts and figures which are given in parentheses.

In the summer of 1922 I was greatly honoured by being invited to be a member of the MCC team that was to tour Australia and New Zealand during the forthcoming winter under the leadership of Archie MacLaren. Archie, of course, captained a team of amateurs that was the first side to beat Warwick Armstrong's Australian team at Eastbourne in 1921, only stressing what a great captain can do when he has the right sort of players to lead.

As I was a serving officer in the Coldstream Guards certain formalities had to be complied with, but as I was at the time serving on the staff of Major-General Sir George Jeffreys at London District all was plain sailing. I knew the General well for I had served in his brigade in France.

No doubt Archie had a good deal to do with the selection of the team and again he pinned his faith on amateurs. Of the fourteen selected twelve were amateurs with 'Tich' Freeman and Harry Tyldesley representing the pros. Our manager was H. D. Swan, President of Essex CCC, who was accompanied by his wife as were MacLaren, myself and Freddy Calthorpe. When the names of the team were published there was a great commotion in New Zealand because some of us had never played in the county championship and the local pundits claimed that we were not good enough to give them a game.

Our programme was to play Western Australia, South Australia, Victoria and New South Wales on our way to New Zealand. Compared with modern touring teams we had a very tough itinerary, for after landing at Freemantle on a Wednesday we were due to play Western Australia on Friday and Saturday. We did play against Ceylon at Colombo but did not have time to win the one-day match. Cricket on a liner at sea is not good practice for the game on terra firma but we did manage to have some practice on the day before we started the match at Perth. Western Australia in those days did not have the standard of player they have today, indeed they were not considered good enough to play in the Sheffield Shield matches. As far as I remember we had the better of the game but no result could be achieved in two days.

Perhaps it was a pity that Archie decided to sail straight on to Adelaide for the crowd would have liked to see him in the field at Perth. However, Archie was looking forward so much to seeing his old friend, Clem Hill, in Adelaide that one cannot blame him too much. Although Clem Hill had retired I think Archie tried to persuade him to play against us at Adelaide. I wish he had succeeded for it would have given us all great pleasure to be on the field with a player described by Sydney Barnes as the greatest batsman he ever bowled against. Barnes told me this when I sat next to him at a dinner at Lord's. I said to him, 'What about Victor Trumper?' to which Barnes replied, 'Ah well! *He* was always giving you a chance.' But for me Victor Trumper was the greatest of them all. Will there ever be another like him? And Sydney Barnes was the greatest right arm bowler I ever played against and 'Charlie' Blythe the greatest left-hander.

So off we went from Perth on what I think was called the 'Transcontinental' train. A very comfortable train it was too, although owing to the differences in the railway gauges we had to change trains five times between Perth and Adelaide. Still, as several of us were interested in the Royal and Ancient game of Bridge we kept ourselves amused. We reached Adelaide again on a Wednesday just in time for a day's practice before the match against South Australia began on Friday. Whether Archie had had any practice before the match I do not know, but in any case he was going to captain us. He lost the toss and the two Richardsons, Arthur and Vic, came in to open the innings – and open it they did in great style. I believe they had put on 300 before we separated them and in the end they made over 600. We succeeded in making them bat again but in the end they beat us by six wickets.

[MacLaren scored 12 and 41 in this game and was given a marvellous reception by the spectators. When he came out to bat in the first innings he was applauded all the way to the wicket and then given three cheers by the South Australian team. The Australian public were amazed that the MCC captain was on his fourth tour yet the last one had been twenty-one years ago!]

On Tuesday we left Adelaide on the Melbourne Express and arrived there the next day giving us a couple of days before the match against Victoria began. We had some practice but although he made a token appearance I don't think Archie had a knock. His old friend, Warwick Armstrong, was taking good care of him, and I don't think it made the slightest difference to Archie whether he practised or not for he was a completely natural player. We lost the match against Victoria by two wickets and if a simple catch had been taken we would probably have won it. Then off we went to Sydney for our match against New South Wales.

[*The Australasian* newspaper commented, 'The placing of the English team was the work of a master and an object lesson to all rising cricketers.']

New South Wales, led by H. L. Collins, had a very strong team of whom only one had not played for his country. We batted first, made 360 and then bowled out the local team for 201. We could have made them follow on but Archie would have none of it, so we batted again and by stumps we were 129 for nine with Archie 28 not out. There can be little doubt that Archie's decision was the right one for the wicket was crumbling, and as he came into the dressing room he said no side could make 150 on that wicket against our bowling. Unfortunately, the groundsman (curator) had the answer to that! There was a very local shower on the Sydney Cricket Ground on the Sunday about twenty-two yards in length and about nine feet in width. When Archie went in on

Monday his partner was quickly dismissed leaving Archie 28 not out. When he got into the dressing room he exploded! The wicket had been watered. As a result NSW had a perfect wicket to bat on and knocked off their 280 runs for the loss of five wickets. However, it was worth watching Charles Macartney making about 80 or 90 of them.

[In the MCC first innings MacLaren renewed his famous record at Sydney by scoring 54. Spectators and players alike were delighted to see the clock turn back to the halcyon days of the Golden Age. The younger element were not to be outdone and it was perhaps fitting that Percy Chapman, one of the few modern batsmen of whom Archie approved, scored 100 in seventy-five minutes. Indeed Chapman had more than fulfilled everybody's hopes, and his brilliant fielding at cover and attacking strokeplay were the undoubted highlight of the tour. In the four games in Australia he scored 75, 58 not out, 32, 53, 73, 69, 100 and 24. This NSW game, although lost, was a great triumph for the unheralded MCC team and much of the credit went to Archie's generalship. The *Sydney Herald* said after the home team had been bowled out for 201, 'MacLaren worked his team with rare judgement, and was accorded a stirring ovation as he returned to the pavilion after the last NSW wicket had fallen.']

After our games in Australia the pundits in New Zealand were not quite so sure that we were not good enough to give them a game. Indeed it may be said now that we never lost a single match in New Zealand.

We were very warmly welcomed in Australia at mayoral receptions and the like but Archie could not be persuaded to reply. Speech-making was not his line but it was very much the line of Swan, our manager, who we thought rather over-bowled himself from time to time. Incidentally we drew good crowds in Australia, rather more than they do today.

There was one thing Archie liked and that was comfort. So when we found ourselves parked in a more or less glorified hut in Sydney we were moved out to Australia Hotel at Archie's behest. In Melbourne, however, all was well for we were put up at Menzies Hotel. Owing to what is now called industrial action, we were held up for a few days in Sydney since the stewards on the ship we were supposed to sail on had gone on strike. Happily, accommodation was found for us in a ship two or three days later and we arrived in Auckland just in time to avoid a change in our programme. In fact the ship we sailed in was very short of stokers, there was another strike, and although some of our team did some stoking we lay becalmed for several hours in the Tasman Sea.

We received a warm welcome in Auckland with the usual receptions but I do not remember Archie replying—Swan did! Our first match against Auckland was rained off but we would surely have won it if not for this. [Archie opened the batting in this match and scored 58 including ten boundaries.]

Before we moved on, the Governor-General, Admiral of the Fleet Earl Jellicoe, gave a delightful party for us at Government House. Archie missed a number of games, and some of the teams we played were very easily beaten, but he stayed in long enough to show what a beautiful player he was.

[Colonel Wilkinson has modestly omitted to mention the game against Canterbury in which he scored 102, putting on 282 in two and a quarter hours with Chapman.]

One game he missed—he may have been sick—was against Wellington on a sticky wicket and we had thirteen against us, eleven in flannels and two in white coats! Thanks to a splendid innings by Titchmarsh we got home by four wickets. It was on this ground that Archie made 200 not out against the full strength of New Zealand and we won by an innings. Anyone who saw that innings of Archie's is never likely to forget it. He went in to bat at lunchtime on the first day and at stumps, 6 pm, he was 162 not out. He continued his innings at 11 am next morning and after half an hour he declared our innings closed, being 200 not out himself. His placing of the ball has never been surpassed. When I was in at the other end there were placed on the off side—mid-off, extra cover, cover point, deep extra cover and deep cover both on the fence as well as a deep third man. Archie managed to hit the ball between them without any of them touching it, mostly along the ground, sometimes in the air. I also distinctly remember him hitting a short ball for six over mid-on's head. Roger Blunt who was fielding at mid-on jumped up and almost managed to catch it, yet it still carried for a six over the spectators' heads. Later on in life I mentioned this incident to Roger Blunt and he confirmed the details of this amazing hit. It was the last innings ever played by Archie in first-class cricket, so he made his exit with bands playing and colours flying.

In conclusion I feel I must refer to Dr Roly Pope, our honorary medical officer, who accompanied the team wherever we went and never failed to administer the right medicine. He too was a very old friend of Archie's.

Colonel Wilkinson was unable to join the rest of the team for the second set of matches in Australia so his interesting reminiscences finish at this point.

The details of Archie's innings in the first of the representative matches against New Zealand are as follows. He came in to bat just before lunch on the first day to a tremendous reception from the crowd of 7,000. With the score at 108 for four he just survived an easy run out chance from his first delivery. After lunch he began hitting out, hooking whenever possible, to reach his 50 in even time and put on 128 in sixty-five minutes for the sixth wicket with Lowry. He then slowed a little giving another run out chance at 80 before reaching a hundred in just over two hours. After this he began to take extravagant risks with the bowling and had scored 162 out of 432 for seven by the close. In all, nine bowlers were tried on the first day, the fielding and bowling being described as pathetic. Next morning he was dropped first ball but went on to score 200 out of 398 in 264 minutes before declaring at 505 for eight. The dispirited New Zealanders were twice bowled out cheaply by Gibson and Freeman to be beaten by an innings with MacLaren taking five catches at slip.

The magnificent six-hit which made such an impression on Alex Wilkinson was described in the *Dominion* newspaper: 'It seemed almost cruel for MacLaren to have extracted a sixer from the ball Garrard sent down, that bounced near the middle of the pitch.' Although the crowd were rapturous when Archie reached his double century, this same newspaper was slightly less generous: 'Contrary to general anticipation, MacLaren did not declare on the resumption of play yesterday morning. Whether he contemplated the prospect of New Zealand getting the runs in their first innings or—as a pavilionite humorously remarked—MacLaren wanted to add yet another 200 to his list and earn a fresh niche in Wisden, was not clear. It is a coincidence that, as soon as his score reached the second century, he immediately closed the innings.'

Despite this sour note almost everybody else was delighted for Archie and the telegrams poured in from all over the world, just as they had twenty-one years previously at Sydney. Especially appreciated were the wishes from old antagonists like Hughie Trumble and Clem Hill. Unfortunately the tremendous effort of Archie's double hundred badly aggravated his old knee injury and he was unable to play again on the tour. In Australia Sir Alan MacCormick x-rayed the knee and advised that further strain would cause a build up of fluid. Archie tried, unsuccessfully, to get fit, but no doubt the fact that the double hundred proved to be his last first-class innings appealed to his sense of the dramatic. He kept up the grand manner to the last. J. C. Hartley captained the team for the rest of the tour which consisted of eleven wins, three draws and no defeats.

On returning to Australia Archie managed to get himself into one of his endless controversies. He had listened to his team being ridiculed by the New Zealand press before the tour, and had been told they would not be able to give the home side a decent game. He then proceeded to thrash the opposition and had been criticised for not going easy with them. Also some of the district and minor matches had been little more than joke games. Instead of letting his deeds on the field speak for him, Archie was reported in the Australian press as saying that the writers in New Zealand ruined the game, that they were ignorant of cricket and that the standard of play was poor with some players hardly knowing one end of a bat from the other. This was unforgiveable behaviour for an MCC captain on a goodwill tour but was nevertheless typical of Archie. If he held an opinion he came straight out with it and let people think what they liked.

Nothing is more certain than the indifference with which MacLaren will have read the reply by the *Dominion* that his criticism was 'ungracious and the remarks in very poor taste, unworthy of the English captain, and gratuitously ill-tempered'. *The Sydney Referee* went further: 'Evidently Mr MacLaren feels at home travelling independently of the team, to judge by this and other experiences since the party left Old England. He thus sets a fashion which, it is hoped, will not be copied by Australians and New Zealanders, who may happen to have the honour of leading touring combinations...Mr MacLaren has not been quite so tactful as a man of his commanding excellence as a cricketer ought to be, to judge by what the Sydney evening papers have regaled their readers with as his views. Naturally, when these were cabled across the Tasman, the New Zealand press hit back in self-defence, as it was bound to . . . Mr MacLaren said that the Dominion scribes of cricket did not understand the game, that in some places where they played, their opponents did not know which end of the bat was the handle, that the public were unappreciative, and that the home cricketers were deficient in certain directions, notably team work . . . There are generally two ways of doing a thing. Unfortunately in this case the captain of the MCC team has chosen the way that will commend itself to few cricketers. It leaves an impression – possibly incorrect – that he has left New Zealand disgruntled.'

The New Zealand cricket council were placated by a letter from MacLaren to their chairman, J. S. Barrett. MacLaren, realising his responsibilities, explained that he had been misquoted and that the press had omitted all the complimentary remarks he had made about the standard of New Zealand cricket. The letter, which was reproduced in the press, was as near to an apology as Archie was ever likely to get. On the team's return to England Lord Harris wrote a letter of congratulation to MacLaren re-assuring him of MCC support. Criticism by the local press, said Harris, 'shows an ignorance of the principles of the game'. One of the more humorous sidelights to this episode occurred shortly afterwards at a local match in New Zealand when a batsman appeared with the handle of his bat clearly indicated by a large label.

To return to the cricket, MCC played four games on their return to Australia, all of which were drawn. They were a much improved team by this time and even had the better of the game with the powerful New South Wales side. Against Victoria, however, they suffered some kind of aberration to find themselves 546 behind on first innings. On the last day, though, Wilson and Hill-Wood batted right through, leaving the score on a most respectable 282 for no wicket. The other highlights of a thoroughly successful tour belonged chiefly to Chapman, Titchmarsh, Wilkinson, Gibson, Freeman and Calthorpe.

The tour was a particularly happy one for Archie and Maud since they were able to celebrate their twenty-fifth wedding anniversary in Australia with their relatives. Memories of that distant tour with Stoddart's team were doubtless evoked and the MCC side presented the couple with a pair of field glasses to commemorate the occasion.

One disappointment for Archie came with the news that Bill Ponsford had eclipsed the record score of 424 which had stood for so long. The MCC team were still in New Zealand when news of the record came through, but since the innings was scored for a Victorian 'second XI' against Tasmania there was some doubt as to its first-class status. When the following year's *Wisden* included Ponsford's score MacLaren was livid and immediately wrote a letter of complaint to S. H. Pardon, the editor. In this letter he outlined his reasons for regarding the match non-first-class and also queried Frank Woolley's 305 not out for MCC against Tasmania in 1911–12. The communication closed thus: 'Without prejudice I am challenging your authority to classify our various games played, and am reporting it to MCC.' Archie's protest was unavailing but he was very upset at losing the record and continued to argue bitterly with Pardon. He recalled that in 1897–8 he had 'lost' his brilliant 181 against a strong NSW/Queensland team because the match was against odds (thirteen men). 'This would have put me top of the first-class averages of the tour (above Ranji), which our XI rather hoped would be the case, but this ruling beat me . . . I never was a record or average hunter, but I do feel it is unfair to get it in the neck both ways.' It is true that MacLaren never batted as if records were important to him, but evidently in his declining years he found it comforting to look back on his greatest innings with a sense of history. However, even Archie must have been satisfied when five years later Ponsford beat the old record again.

To return to the tour, when the team was on the return journey the Lancashire club received a cablegram which read, 'Please post £50 to Port Said to enable overland tour – MacLaren.' The committee, by now rather exasperated by such requests, replied, 'Regret committee cannot accede to your request.' Whether this left Mr and Mrs MacLaren stranded in Port Said or not we shall never know, but by 4 May Sir Edwin Stockton was able to reveal to the Lancashire committee that he had agreed a sum of £105 in termination of the club's proposed agreement for MacLaren to continue as coach in 1923. He added that it was by no means certain MacLaren would not make a further application for money! The club minutes recorded with an air of gratitude, 'A unanimous vote of thanks was passed to Sir Edwin for the very able manner in which he had dealt with the whole business.'

Johnny Tyldesley was appointed coach for 1923 at a salary of £300 per annum, £250 less than MacLaren's. The press were tactfully informed that it was Archie's knee injury which precluded his continuing in the post. Len Hopwood recalled MacLaren's departure from Old Trafford: 'The news that he was to leave Old Trafford was a shock to the young players, but it was inevitable I suppose. MacLaren was by nature intended to be master, never servant. There must have been innumerable clashes of will between committee and coach. Never will I forget his final words on the subject. ''The Lancashire committee mustn't think they own me body and soul because they pay me a paltry £550 a year.'' This sum of money was not to be sniffed at fifty years ago, particularly by one whom it was rumoured was not exactly riding on the crest of a financial wave. But MacLaren was no ordinary mortal.'

Not exactly on the crest of a financial wave sums up fairly accurately Archie's life for the next fifteen years after his active cricket career finished. There were periods of ups and downs, the peaks usually due to occasional windfalls from Maud's Australian family, and the troughs invariably following one of Archie's abortive money-making schemes. During this period MacLaren gained something of a reputation for running up debts and borrowing money from his friends. Those who were close to him, however, knew that he was never a mean scrounger (unlike some famous cricketers) but just the opposite. Patrick Morrah tells a delightful story which captures perfectly the generous side of Archie's nature as well as his hopelessness with money. Once during a particularly difficult financial period Archie received a much-needed cheque for some hack reporting he had done for a newspaper. His immediate reaction was to use the money to hire a hotel room and to invite all his old cricketing friends for a drink, doubtless to listen to stories of the strategy employed in bygone Test matches. This was very much true to type for Archie had no idea whatsoever about money. If he had money he spent it lavishly and if he didn't have any he saw no harm in accepting other people's. The local pub grew accustomed to two very different Archies: one week it might be champagne all round and the next it would be half of bitter on the slate.

Although he was often a generous and straightforward man he sometimes, usually through carelessness, let people down rather badly, especially in financial matters. There was the Pentelow incident concerning *The World of Cricket*, also the large champagne bill that was left unpaid when he left Old Trafford in 1923 – and these were far from being the only cases.

How then did the family manage in the inter-war years with no reliable income? The answer lay in numerous magazine and newspaper articles and in a variety of business ventures which filled the gaps in Maud's money. Archie's regular reporting of Test matches made him a familiar figure on the leading grounds where he would be found continuously talking cricket to anybody who would listen. The cartoon by his very close friend, Tom Webster, which is reproduced here, typifies the affectionate reputation he had in the cricketing world. In 1930 MacLaren also made several radio broadcasts concerning the Tests. Doubtless these were outspoken and full of tactical minutiae but unfortunately the recordings no longer exist.

Like many an old cricketer he was generally critical of the current generation. One of his pet complaints, as in 1921, was that youth should be given more of a chance. He argued that although many batsmen in their thirties or forties could reel off strings of centuries in county cricket, they did not have the extra sharpness to deal with the likes of Gregory and McDonald. In addition, this brought down the general level of fielding. One notable exception in MacLaren's eyes was Jack Hobbs. The regard in which Archie

Silence Is Still Golden   By TOM WEBSTER

THE HEAT
MATCH
MANCHESTER
MONDAY

SITTING

AND

SEETHING ON THE RIM OF
THE CAULDRON AT OLD TRAFFORD
WE HAVE HAD A SPLENDID
TIME TO·DAY

ARCHIE McCLAREN WAS IMMEDIATELY
BEHIND US AND WHEN MR MACLAREN
BEGINS TO TALK ABOUT CRICKET IT
REALLY DOESN'T MATTER WHETHER YOU
ARE IN FRONT OF HIM OR BEHIND HIM.

FROM 11·0AM UNTIL
LUNCH TIME MR MACLAREN

IN A SHORT DISCOURSE
OF THREE MILLION
WORDS TOLD US ABOUT EVERY
TEST MATCH SINCE 1884.

THROWING CONSONANTS AT US
THAT BURNT LIKE HOT COALS
MR MACLAREN WAS SO
DESCRIPTIVE THAT WE

FELT WE WERE
NEARLY IN THE
MATCHES
OURSELVES AND

ONCE
WITH
HIS
STEADY
DRONE
WE
WERE
ALMOST
ASLEEP
AND RUNNING TO THE
BOUNDARY IN 1901.

WHEN
WE
LEFT
THE GROUND AT 5·0 P.M.

EVERYBODY WAS
TALKING ABOUT THE
GREAT FIGHT THE
AUSTRALIANS WERE PUTTING UP

THAT'S ALL VERY
WELL. THEY MAY BE
ABLE TO BATTLE
AGAINST OUR BOWLERS
BUT LET 'EM LISTEN
TO ARCHIE MACLAREN
FOR 5 HOURS.

Tom Webster

Archie was a favourite character in Tom Webster's sporting cartoons which
appeared for many years in the *Daily Mail*. This one, which appeared on 10 July
1934, captures beautifully MacLaren's abilities as a talker.

159

held Hobbs is demonstrated by the fact that he compiled a full length book devoted to a study of 'The Master', including a series of still photographs taken from cine film. Archie's other theories regarding the state of cricket technique were thoroughly expounded in another book published two years previously. Most controversial of the points raised in this work was MacLaren's suggestion that the googly should be banned.

By way of contrast, when bodyline was exploited by Jardine in 1932—3 Archie was dogmatic that the tactics were perfectly fair. In the *News of the World* he wrote: 'Certain bowlers have bowled at my body viciously in the past, and just as viciously have I deflected the balls to the boundary behind short leg, or stepped back for a full swing to clip them in front of short leg, always remaining sideways in making the strokes. No vicious bowler ever hit me and I never in my life ducked my head to any bowler. I have never for one moment in my life thought an Australian tried to, or ever wished to, hit me, but that Cotter bowled at my body to force me to play the red, swinging ball goes without saying. They were very clever and perfectly legitimate tactics on his part.'

With the Australians squealing at a drop of fast bowling, doubtless this was just the kind of stirring stuff people wanted to see in their Sunday papers. Archie, though, was not in Australia in 1932—3, and the consensus of opinion of those who were would seem to suggest that bodyline by Larwood to a packed legside field was a very different proposition from anything that had gone before. On the other hand, Cotter was a very fast, wild and sometimes vicious bowler and MacLaren did indeed deal with him in just the manner he describes.

Once during the winter when the bodyline controversy was at its peak MacLaren was being driven through London in a taxi. By chance he happened to notice his old crony Gerry Weigall walking by and immediately ordered the cabby to stop. Archie then proceeded to describe through the window exactly how he would have played the short pitched balls of Larwood—apparently only MacLaren was oblivious of the fact that they were at one of the busiest crossings in Piccadilly and there was a mass of blaring motor horns behind them.

Weigall was a very close friend and accomplice of Archie and, just as with Walter Brearley, they were a great double act. Both Gerry and Archie were experts at the extended monologue, usually concerning cricket, and to hear them both in full flow, playing off each other in turn, was apparently a seldom forgotten experience. They could usually talk their way into or out of anything. Weigall was just as well-loved as Archie but equally impecunious, and friends who saw the pair dining together would often be curious as to who, if either of them, was paying the bill.

During the early twenties MacLaren used to make quite a sum of money from coaching – not the type of appointment usually taken on by an old professional but at large exclusive stores like Harrod's. For a week of lecturing and instruction he would be paid the not inconsiderable sum of fifty guineas plus expenses and commission on goods sold. Apparently such cricket weeks could increase substantially the sales made to local schools. Tied in with these ventures was the marketing of a cricket bat designed by MacLaren and the showing of films that he had commissioned. These included films of the 1924 South Africans and some fascinating footage of Jack Hobbs playing in 1914. What has become of this invaluable archive material remains a mystery. MacLaren made quite a business of hiring these films out to schools and even negotiated distribution rights with a gentleman in Scotland; he could certainly be an inventive and persevering business man, though never a successful one. One amusing business letter starts by requesting £100 for a sole film agency, then proceeds to apologise for the fact that the horse racing selections in his last letter 'were so wide of the mark'.

There were numerous other projects and schemes during these years. At one time the MacLarens bought a hotel only to find that business fell off owing to Archie's habit of being extremely rude to any guest he did not like the look of. MacLaren's son, Ian, who shared many of Archie's interests and closely resembled his father, became a partner in a number of unproductive businesses the most striking of which must have been the 'Ormonde Bloodstock Agency'. Ormonde was one of the greatest classic-winning colts in the history of racing but unfortunately he was a failure at stud. Archie's bloodstock venture which bore the horse's name was equally ill-fated since it did not manage to produce a single foal.

As far as cricket was concerned Archie played very little after the New Zealand tour. The occasional club or country house match was all he could fit in around his journalistic and other activities. In 1924 he appeared in the Eastbourne Cricket Week mainly to accompany his two sons, neither of whom really shared their father's love of or ability for the game. As if to show that he could still pick up a bat with no practice and score in his old style, he made a sparkling 86 in a high-class two-day club fixture. Much of this innings was made in partnership with K. S. Duleepsinhji, nephew of Archie's great friend of the Golden Age, Ranji. The fortunate few spectators at the Saffrons that day must surely have reflected on perhaps the last link between the elegant days of Victorian cricket and the modern game. How many of them realised that the talented Duleep had not been born until ten years *after* Archie had made his monumental 424?

In the winter of 1924–5 MacLaren acted as manager of a private cricket tour of South Africa by Mr S. B. Joel's XI. Known as the 'Jolly Souls' this team was a very strong combination and included J. C. W. MacBryan, G. Geary, E. Tyldesley and Lionel Tennyson who captained the side. Archie did not play in any of their matches but he did take part in a local club game in which he captained one team and gave some coaching. This tour was really the end of Archie's formal association with cricket other than as a critic.

The final important event in Archie's life occurred shortly before the outbreak of the Second World War. Maud at last received a very large inheritance from her family in Australia and there was enough to ensure that the now elderly couple could live out their last days in comfort and ease. Archie was still active and although he walked with a stick and suffered from his old aches and pains, he retained his lively interest in racing, coursing and motor cars, as well as cricket. The bulk of the legacy was spent on a grand new home for the family. The site chosen was Warfield Park, near Bracknell in Berkshire, a large estate of over 150 acres containing an ancient mansion house and several cottages. Significantly, Ascot race course was only a stone's throw away. This beautiful part of the country had been the favourite haunt of the MacLarens who had lived in several different houses in the area over the years. The newly acquired mansion, though, was in a totally uninhabitable, tumbledown condition and Archie immediately proceeded to have a new house built on the estate. When completed the magnificent new home was affectionately named Myrnong after Maud's birthplace.

It was about this time that Archie went on a trip to America and visited his old friend, Sir Charles Aubrey Smith, one time England cricketer but now a Hollywood movie star. Known as 'Round the Corner' in his cricketing days, owing to his manner of bowling, Smith always maintained his interest in cricket and cricketers and welcomed Archie with open arms. During the course of the visit, as well as the interminable reminiscing that surely occurred, Archie was persuaded to take a small role in Smith's latest film, *The Four Feathers* starring Smith and Ralph Richardson and to be released by United Artists in 1939. MacLaren appeared as a Crimea war veteran and was paid the princely sum of two guineas for two days work. If this ancient film has ever appeared as a fill-in for an unpopular time-slot on television, one wonders whether even the most enthusiastic of cricket followers would have realised that he was watching two former England cricket captains of the Golden Age.

The MacLarens spent a happy few years at Warfield Park despite the onset of the war, and with no financial troubles Archie could entertain his friends as he had always wished. After a few years, though, Archie's health began to deteriorate and a car crash did not help matters. Finally, on 17 November 1944, two weeks before his seventy-third birthday, Archie died of cancer. The loss proved too much for Maud, who was devoted to the husband she had first met fifty years earlier; she declined rapidly and died only a few months later. In spite of the impending victory over Germany which dominated the news, MacLaren's passing did not go unnoticed and many tributes were paid in the press. The funeral was attended by F. S. Jackson, P. F. Warner, H. D. G. Leveson-Gower, and J. R. Mason amongst others.

12

The Style is the Man

'Magnificence was enthroned at the wicket when MacLaren took his stand there and surveyed the field with a comprehensive eye. I thrill to this day at the very thought of his perpetual aspect of mastery.'

Sir Neville Cardus

Such nostalgic memories of cricketers in the Golden Age are prompted not by the number of runs they scored but by the graceful and dashing style of their batting. The old writers, such as the incomparable Cardus, wax lyrical over Spooner, Palairet, Ranji or Mason. Their batting was a classical and beautiful art, painstakingly learnt at the public schools and developed on the much improved pitches of the late nineteenth century. MacLaren's method of play rightly places him on the same lofty pedestal as these famous stylists, but despite his reputation for possessing the grand manner he was more akin to C. B. Fry, a far less flowery player than many contemporaries. Fry, an astute observer of technique, recognised this when assessing Archie's style: 'His style in batting is an example of the perfect adaptation of means to ends. He is not a batsman with striking peculiarities or distinguishing strokes. He is too good for that.' Also Cardus himself assures us that, 'His cricket was based on science; he was a sound player first and last.' The Hon. R. H. Lyttelton, writing before MacLaren had reached his peak, goes even further: 'He is not a player gifted with

164

any one particular hit, but . . . is altogether a thrusting sort of player with no striking grace of style.'

For detailed descriptions of MacLaren's batting technique we must amass the evidence quoted by those who saw him. Frequently this leads us to Fry or Cardus, but an equally valuable source is to be found in Monty Noble's perceptive autobiography. Noble certainly had enough opportunities to study MacLaren's stance at the wicket: 'MacLaren's stand at the wickets when batting was peculiar and entirely his own. First he would place his right foot in position and put his bat very carefully into the block; then he would take up position with legs slightly apart, and at the same time up would go his chin, as though he were saying to the bowler, ''Now, bring out your cat''.'

One of the reasons for MacLaren's impression of grandeur at the wicket was undoubtedly his extraordinary backlift and full swing of the bat. As he stood waiting for the bowler he held the bat high above his head like a golfer at the top of his swing. The resultant downward swing provided tremendous power for all his shots, not only drives. It was often said that a feature of his play and the main reason for his fast scoring rate was the ability to force a good length ball for runs. The secret of this was not only the high backlift but also the way in which he could play forward 'on the up'. The fact that this is a far less risky business in Australia than in England may partly account for his success there.

Cardus perfectly captured the sense of majesty: 'I can still see the swing of MacLaren's bat, the great follow-through, finishing high and held there with the body poised as he himself contemplated the grandeur of the stroke and savoured it.' Certainly MacLaren's batting was majestic, but it also had an uncompromising quality. This impression was gained because he either played right forward by taking a long stride, or right back on his stumps with an exaggerated study of the ball. As C. B. Fry observed, 'He never hedged on his stroke; he never pulled his punches.' The dominating forward stroke which sent even the good length ball for runs was described by Fry as a 'full-fledged swinging lunge'. More strikingly, Cardus averred, 'You have never seen a player play forward if you never saw MacLaren.' Nevertheless, as with so many of the 'greats', Archie's special ability as a batsman lay in his strong backfoot play. The imperious cover drive may have caught the eye but, as MacLaren himself put it, 'Any fool can play forward, but it is only the good player who can score off forceful back strokes.' Jessop commented, 'In his way, Mr MacLaren in back play was as great a genius as Arthur Shrewsbury. He always seemed to have more time in which to execute this stroke than the ordinary individual.'

This policy of playing either well forward or well back accounts for his success on sticky wickets where the ball 'pops' or spins unpredictably. In these circumstances Archie would step forward boldly to drive any delivery that was pitched up and retreat right back onto his stumps for any of a shorter length. His neatness and speed of foot, which were remarkable for such a big man, enabled him quickly to adopt the perfect position for either of these eventualities. Monty Noble noted this capacity when commenting, 'MacLaren's recovery was so quick, his anticipation so sure, and his defence so extraordinary that his legs were rarely hit at all.'

As regards the individual types of attacking stroke most emphasis has usually been placed on MacLaren's driving, but his peculiar glory and his most productive strokes were the hook and pull shots. Beldam and Fry's standard text on players of this era curiously makes no reference to MacLaren's hook, but there is no doubt that it was as famous on the cricket grounds of the day as were Spooner's cover drive or Ranji's leg glance. Again, Noble describes perfectly the manner in which the stroke was played: 'The shot I admired most of all was his pull stroke off a ball just short of a good length and rising rapidly. He would be upright in a twinkling, pivoting on his right foot and, as the stroke was made, would turn on it and force the ball into just the position he desired, beating the fieldsman by playing it between them or making a safe half-stroke over their heads into the country.' An excellent description of the technique is, fortunately for those who never saw MacLaren, given life by one of Cardus' most famous sentences: 'To see MacLaren hook a fast ball—especially a fast ball of Ernest Jones—from the front of his face, was in those days an experience which thrilled me like heroic poetry; he didn't merely hook the ball, he dismissed it from his presence.'

Gilbert Jessop once told the story of one of MacLaren's hundreds at Sydney when W. P. Howell plotted to curb this devastating hook shot. He began bowling with two fielders carefully placed in the region of deep square leg. By the end of the innings the hapless bowler had five men there.

So much for the style and the strokes, but what of the tactics and strategy of an innings? Basically, MacLaren believed implicitly that the initiative should be taken out of the bowler's hands. It was this that made him such a match-winner. 'He batted on his own terms; he would not compromise at the behest of anybody, let his name be Lockwood, Trumble, Noble or Hirst.'—Cardus. 'Like all great batsmen, he always attacked the bowling.' — Fry. Sometimes Archie would indulge his taste for gambling in his desire to take the initiative. Once in a Test match at Sydney, Joe Darling opened the England innings with a ring of fielders blocking Archie's productive leg-side strokes. In the very first over of the game MacLaren, the England captain, drove good length balls from Ernest Jones straight back for four and forced Darling to open up the field. His positive tactics had paid off and allowed the rest of the innings to proceed more comfortably.

MacLaren's batting is legendary but it is perhaps less well known that he was also one of the leading fieldsmen of the day. In his youth he was a marvellously quick and sure outfielder, usually to be seen at third man or deep square leg. Some of his athletic stops and catches in these positions were famous and reference has already been made to the historic effort in the Gentlemen v. Players match of 1899. As the nineteenth century closed and Archie became an established captain it was necessary for him to field closer to the wicket. His natural athleticism and eye for the ball made the transition to slip a straightforward one and soon the position had become his own. During this period the greatest slip fielders were MacLaren, Braund, A. O. Jones and Ranji. When any three of these were in the same England XI the bowlers had few opportunities to curse their luck. Beldam and Fry's book on great

167

batsmen contains some fascinating photographs of Braund and MacLaren in the slips to Lockwood's bowling during the famous Oval Test of 1902. Braund is very fine at first slip and is standing fully upright in a casual manner even though the ball is halfway down the wicket. Archie, on the other hand, can be seen at a wide third slip position crouched low with both hands reaching forward much as Neville Cardus remembered. 'He would fastidiously pick his trousers at the knees and bend down, arms outstretched—not ravenously outstretched, not craving a catch, but waiting for one, as his due. When a snick sped to him from a fast bowler, MacLaren descended on it and the ball was thrown high in the air with the same action that had scooped it up, an eighth of an inch from the turf—a great swift circling action, momentous and thrilling. MacLaren never looked to see where the ball went after he had thrown it high over his shoulders.'

MacLaren was certainly a very great batsman and fielder but his prominent position in cricket's history owes just as much to his reputation as a captain. The leading captains of the past have been the subject of books and the changing role of the captain has been discussed in depth. In addition the necessary qualities have been outlined in numerous instructional and biographical publications, but inevitably a conclusive assessment of the relative merits of different captains has proved elusive. It is only in relatively recent years that a captain's every decision has come under close scrutiny by press and television. Well into the present century reports of matches contain scant reference to tactics and strategy or even sometimes to the identity of the captain. It was around the turn of the century that captaincy assumed any major importance, coincident with the increased interest in Test cricket and the rise of the Golden Age. A new generation of tactically aware leaders emerged in the persons of MacLaren, Warner, Trott, Darling and Noble. These were the first of the modern-style captains typified in later times by such as Bradman and Benaud. Until these players arrived on the scene little thought was given to matters such as varying the field setting or batting order to suit different conditions. Such aspects of the game were far more stereotyped in the nineteenth century.

In order to assess MacLaren's strengths and weaknesses as a captain it may be useful to define those areas in which a captain's influence is felt.

Team Selection. This is the basis upon which a match can be won or lost. The optimum composition of a team can depend on many factors including the particular opposition strengths, whether an attacking or consolidating policy is required, or the likely state of the wicket. Curiously the captain has often had little say in matters of team selection.

Tactics and Strategy. Once the selected team takes the field there is endless tactical scope for a captain to alter the course of a match. Examples include field placing, bowling changes, batsmen's weaknesses, attack or defence, batting order, declarations and putting the opposition in to bat first.

Psychology. This aspect of leadership encompasses the captain's interaction with his own team and with the opposition. He must be popular with, win the respect of, and motivate his own players. A side with few outstanding individuals can often play consistently above itself if a winning mood can be obtained. Perhaps even more difficult, the captain must be able to pick a beaten side up off the floor. Regarding the opposition, pressurising one's opponent is now an accepted part of all professional sport. Television may have recently drawn attention to the particular type of 'needle' associated with modern Test matches but fielding sides have been generating uncomfortable atmospheres for many years before that.

Luck. Under this vital heading we must include the toss, the weather and injuries, all of which can undo the most perfectly captained teams.

Now perhaps the question can be answered, how good a captain was MacLaren? Opinions concerning this point have been sharply divided over the years. Some critics insist he was indisputably the finest captain ever whereas others aver that his faults far outweighed his strengths. Certainly all would agree that his captaincy was never dull. Controversy, as has been seen throughout this book, was never far away.

Perhaps the greatest of these controversies, particularly in Test cricket, arose from the vexed question of team selection. On many occasions during the ten years (1899–1909) which spanned Archie's England leadership, inexplicable or unbalanced sides were chosen by the newly formed selection committee. This committee, chaired by Lord Hawke, sought advice from prominent amateur cricketers and usually from the England captain, but it is wrong to assume that MacLaren had a particularly influential voice in such matters. Although he would often get his own way with regard to a particular favourite cricketer, such as Young in 1899, Barnes in 1902 at Sheffield and Sharp in 1909, the committee always had the last word and there were many examples of MacLaren being exasperated at the composition of his team, the most famous case being the Fred Tate match. A different character might have accepted what he was given and knuckled down to making the best of it, but Archie could not hide his feelings over such matters. It was for this reason that he was often labelled a pessimistic captain who considered himself beaten before the match even began. This is a misinterpretation of the truth. Archie did not take umbrage merely because he could not have his own way. The reason he showed his disappointment with many bad selections was simply that he cared passionately, almost frantically, that England should beat Australia. Many amateurs of the day found it impossible to comprehend the depth to which Archie was consumed by every tiny detail and facet of what was to him a campaign of war.

A perfect example of this is provided by Pelham Warner, a splendid captain in his own right but a person who just was not on the same wavelength as MacLaren. 'He (MacLaren) was rather faddy in the actual choosing of a team', wrote Warner, 'being apt to run away with some theory about a particular cricketer.' This statement is perfectly accurate but MacLaren would have regarded it as a compliment rather than the intended criticism. One need only cite the solitary occasion when MacLaren had sole responsibility for selecting the England team—the tour to Australia in 1901–2. Although England were heavily defeated, MacLaren pulled off the greatest selection coup of all time in the shape of

Sydney Barnes—'a rather faddy theory'. The previously untried Blythe and Braund were also 'theories' that MacLaren 'ran away with'.

The simple answer to the criticism that MacLaren was a poor captain because he could not agree with his selectors is that he was usually correct. He was simply a better and more experienced judge of a cricketer than most of his contemporaries. He was correct when he said Jessop should be an automatic selection. He was right about Barnes. He was right about Fred Tate and he was right about the young players needed to beat Armstrong's 1921 Australians. To be fair, Archie made his fair share of selectoral mistakes, the most serious being the omission of a fast bowler at the Oval in 1909. It is true, however, that many similar decisions, e.g. Lord's 1909, were popularly attributed to MacLaren when in fact he had no part in them.

There may have been some dispute about MacLaren's ability to select a team, but there has always been unanimous agreement that he had no peer when it came to tactical matters on the field of play. Of all those who played either under or against Archie's captaincy perhaps the two most discerning students of cricket technique were C. B. Fry and M. A. Noble. Their opinions regarding MacLaren effectively settle the issue. Noble—'MacLaren was a wonderful judge of the game and a master of field placing. He could estimate an opponent's strength and ferret out his weakness with great accuracy, and, what is more, he knew the right kind of bowler to put on to take advantage of his knowledge.' And Fry—'He certainly had no superior, to say the least, as a tactician. When you play against Lancashire you feel at once that you are playing against a brain . . . MacLaren plays his cricket as a kind of athletic chess, grasping the condition of wicket and weather almost ere he has left the pavilion, and moving his men down to the smallest pawn, with consummate resource.'

Whatever the majesty and grandeur of MacLaren's batting, it was as a leader in the field that he really stood supreme. This exercise in 'athletic chess' was the one activity in Archie's varied life that saw him pre-eminent. Modern cricketers, well versed in the one-day game, doubtless consider they have developed the art of field placing to the ultimate, but never has anyone put more thought or planning into deployment of troops than did MacLaren. He pioneered the now commonplace practice of blocking a batsman's favourite shots. Like a general he would survey the field from slip, making minor changes to suit a particular batsman or tactical situation. Every man in the team was under strict orders to watch MacLaren at such times for the subtlest of instructions – deep long-off could be moved ten yards either way merely by a flicking gesture of MacLaren's boot. He could bellow across the field or wave theatrically if he chose, but the changes that mattered were conspicuous only when the batsman was on his way back to the pavilion.

This skill at managing a fielding side was largely the result of Archie's tremendously varied experience. To some extent, though, the ability came naturally to him. Jessop remembered the young MacLaren when he first captained Lancashire: 'A very boyish-looking figure ... but very long-headed even then in the management of men in the field.'

One of Archie's pet tactical theories was that in every well fought game there came a critical moment when the tide was turning and if a captain missed this moment then all could be lost. This matter of the timing of a change in tactics raises the one point on which MacLaren could be faulted. Noble remarked: 'If there was a weakness in his method of general attack it was a tendency to give his stock bowler too long a spell at the crease.' This was not carelessness but a genuine tactic. He felt that a tiring front-line bowler was a more likely weapon than a fresh change bowler who was not in the same class. Examples of this were provided by Archie's merciless use of Barnes in 1901 – 2 and Carr in 1909. On balance the success of change bowlers over the years proved him wrong, but where the theory really cost dearly was when Barnes broke down due to overbowling. The practice was fine, though, with bowlers like Brearley and Braund and indeed these were the type of performers that MacLaren preferred.

The third category of leadership, psychology, provides both a weakness and a strength in MacLaren's armoury. Archie was a pastmaster at making the opposition feel inferior and uncomfortable, but unfortunately he also had this effect on his own team at times. Everything in Archie's bearing, in cricket and in everyday life, radiated superiority. When he batted, he was the one who dominated proceedings, but equally he was determined that the roles would be reversed when he was in the field. Percy Cross Standing observed: 'Marshalled by MacLaren, Lancashire's fielding ever frowned at you: if possible you shall not be spared. He created an atmosphere of hostility, this captain; well-mannered and decent hostility, but penetrative into the marrow of the batsman. A determined, incisive captain, MacLaren; with an encyclopaedia of cricket up his sleeve. And his fieldsmen follow his lead.' Such an attitude, chilling as it was for a batsman, could rebound if members of one's own team were not like-minded. C. B. Fry told Denzil Batchelor that MacLaren was 'an iron and joyless captain ... under him you entered every game bowed down with the Herculean labour of a cricket match against Australia; you went as in a trance to your doom.' This 'iron and joyless' attitude would be regarded as competitive and professional today.

The one overwhelming criticism levelled at MacLaren's captaincy was that he was a pessimist. Perhaps this was due to his serious disposition and rigid discipline on the field which could give the impression that he felt all was far from well. P. F. Warner, who always appeared genial himself, was one who interpreted MacLaren this way, despite the fact that he played only once under his captaincy in a Test. The idea that MacLaren was a cricketing pessimist has become accepted as fact largely on Warner's evidence. Indeed, an overwhelming proportion of the adverse criticism levelled at MacLaren's leadership came from the pen of Warner; written long after both men had finished playing, it was partly responsible for a decline in MacLaren's reputation as an England captain. This change during the interwar years would have been unthinkable to cricket enthusiasts during the Golden Age, who had generally placed Archie at the top of the list.

There is, of course, some truth in such criticism. Archie was certainly pessimistic about his luck—with some justification—and he was prone to be critical rather than helpful when things were going badly. On the other hand, we have A. F. A. Lilley's testimony that during the 1901—2 tour, when everything went wrong, 'Mr MacLaren was never depressed'. Any individual's opinion of Archie as a captain really depended on how they reacted to his complex and unusual personality. One man might find him joyless while another would be devoted. In general he certainly commanded respect from those under his leadership, particularly the professionals. On balance we should perhaps conclude that he was too inflexible to suit everyone that played under him.

It appears that in his later years his attitude on the field may have mellowed slightly, although the youngsters at Old Trafford in 1922 knew what to expect if they failed to toe the line. Those who played under him after the war, particularly at Eastbourne, express nothing but admiration for him, quoting especially his optimism and imperturbability.

Finally, regarding the matter of luck, the way in which fate ran against Archie became a byword. Incapacitating injuries during vital matches—Barnes, Briggs, Jessop—cost him more dearly than anyone before or since. Also control of the rain and sun remained forever outside his capabilities. The only aspect at which he could maintain at least parity with nature was in the toss; in twenty-two Test matches as captain he won the toss exactly eleven times. Archie himself concluded cynically that luck was the real secret of leadership: 'It's easy to get a reputation for omniscient captaincy if the other side is not too good,' he once remarked.

Two of Archie's greatest cricketing friends from his heyday as captain of Lancashire and England paid him the following tributes: 'In my opinion he was not only the greatest captain ever, but was always a valued friend and adviser to the youthful cricketer during early appearances for the county.'—Reggie Spooner. 'I shall always say I have never met a better captain.'—Walter Brearley. Amongst the younger generation who played at Eastbourne: 'He made a great impression on me both as a man and as an astute and imperturbable captain.'—Gilbert Ashton. 'He was the finest captain I

ever played under.' –George Wood. Alex Wilkinson summed up
the opinion of many when he said, 'It might fairly be said that
Archie was not quite all the same to all men, but all the members of
our team were devoted to him. We were enthralled by his superb
technique and his shrewd leadership, but there may have been
times when he was a little awkward.' Again, Sir Hubert Ashton
noted, 'Archie was a fine, handsome man of strong character and it
was inevitable that he did not get on with everybody. He impressed
us young men and gave us a sense of confidence tinged with awe.'

Finally, this biography ends with Archie's own assessment of
Victor Trumper, the prince of Australian batsmen. In many ways
this brief quote captures the true character of MacLaren: 'Myself, I
was considered out of a good stable. They talked of my grand
manner. Well, compared to Victor, I was an honest selling plater in
the company of a Derby thoroughbred.'

Appendix A

W. G. Grace – An Appreciation by A. C. MacLaren

On 25 October 1935, MacLaren broadcast an appreciation of W. G. Grace on BBC Radio. The script, written by Archie, is reproduced here for the first time.

W. G. GRACE

My first introduction to W. G. Grace took place in the Old Trafford pavilion and I well remember watching the great man tying his MCC sash round his waist, as I gazed in admiration at what appeared to me to be a very genial Father Christmas with a black beard. He was of massive proportions and was more suited to the role of Father Christmas than of a great cricketer. The whole place was alive with merriment, as was always the case when W.G. was present. He put out an enormous paw, saying: ''Ow are you, little man?' and then continued his chaff surrounded by Lancashire members and one or two players.

So inspired was I by this great man's presence, that when my father said: 'Now, my boy, you have seen the captain of England', I informed my mother that some day I also would be captain of England when I grew up. It was an extraordinary coincidence that he should have wired to me at the end of his Test cricket career to take his place as captain.

I had played under W.G. on the previous visit of the Australians, and my affection for this dear old man was such that it inspired my own cricketing ability. For I could not have wished to serve under a more encouraging, sympathetic and appreciative captain. There was always the feeling on my part of complete security, whenever I had the good fortune to be one of his team. The delight expressed by him on every occasion, at anything out of the ordinary, on the part of the fieldsmen, acted as an incentive to every man to produce his best. Indeed, I will go further—the winning atmosphere his presence created seemed to make everyone produce *more* than his best.

For some reason a certain few held the opinion that W.G. was not as good a captain as would be expected. This was not my view. In all the matches I played with or against him I can think of no occasion on which adverse criticism would have been justified. He invited most generously valued opinion. I ought to make it clear to my listeners that I was too young ever to have seen the Champion at the zenith of his career—in those years when one *can* only be at one's best—for he was distinctly an old man for a Test cricketer when I first played under him.

This, however, did not prevent him from being top scorer in one of the three Test matches in which I played under his captaincy; and again in Gentlemen v. Players match at Lord's on his fiftieth birthday against the cream of English bowling, on a difficult wicket—a really wonderful performance.

We all know that as a batsman his methods were of the soundest, with every stroke on the board at his command, while his concentration was most marked. An outstanding feature was the accuracy with which he placed the ball between the fieldsmen, particularly in the cutting strokes through the slips. One can truthfully say that on all wickets and against every type of bowling he remained supreme. I once asked him which bowler he liked least of all. He paused for a moment, then rapped out: 'Archie, I love 'em all!'

W.G. practised assiduously and seldom missed a short spell at the nets before the day's play commenced, firstly for the purpose of getting his eye accustomed to the prevailing light and secondly to enable him to loosen his shoulders for the production of that delightfully even flow of strokes that was to follow in the game and was his trade-mark from start to finish of his career. No batsman ever produced with greater regularity a stroke to every type of ball than W.G., who seldom was seen to leave a ball alone. That great wicket-keeper, Blackham, who captained Australia on my first visit in '94, said that W.G. practically never allowed him to take a ball behind the wickets when he was batting. W.G. aimed at harassing the bowler throughout, employing orthodox methods to such purpose that the bowler was soon wishing he could have an extra fieldsman or two. Such is only possible when all the strokes are produced, which should be the aim of every batsman.

People have asked if W.G. ever appeared to be nervous, and on my referring this question to him, he replied: 'Well, I always feel better after my luncheon.' Certainly his play gave no indication that he was ever nervous. He demonstrated to all of us that wet wickets and hard wickets all came alike to him. Which reminds me of an amusing incident that took place before my playing days—when Yorkshire were playing Gloucestershire. W.G., whilst batting, was handed a telegram, which in those days was always brought out to the player on the field. Tom Emmett, the left-hand bowler—a rare Yorkshire character—appeared to be interested. W.G. called out to him: 'I've got my diploma, Tom.' Shortly after W.G. slipped and sat on the muddy wicket to hear Tom call out, as he picked himself up: 'Ah see thoist got diploma all right, Doctor.'

W.G. was always held up as a true model of physical fitness, and my mother was the first to tell me that he neither drank nor smoked, but it was not long before I had good reason to doubt the accuracy of my mother's statement, for I now frequently had the opportunity of seeing for myself. Certainly he was most careful of his diet, but on one occasion after a long innings, when, as often, he was the guest of the evening, one of his team noticing he had gone beyond his two glasses of champagne, remarked to him: 'I thought you said, W.G., you never had more than two glasses of wine at dinner?' 'Ted', replied W.G., 'I said I could drink any *given* quantity.' The very soundness of his successes left no room for any lack of confidence in himself at any time, even when age was overtaking him. This he showed in his reply to my expression of sorrow at an unusually early return to the pavilion after opening the innings against Australia—'There's a record innings yet, Archie.'

Another saying never to be forgotten by cricketers and which should still give all food for thought, came from him. 'The beauty of this game lies in the knowledge that there is always something to be learnt every day you play it', and this from the Champion of Champions.

In these days when accidents to batsmen appear to be rather more frequent than formerly, it will not surprise my listeners to hear that I can't remember ever seeing W.G. hit by the ball, let alone hurt, and I might also add that he never missed a match through ill-health.

A. N. Hornby, my first captain, a great one, and a fine international player, told me of an occasion when owing to lack of accommodation he shared a bedroom with W.G. As he opened the door in the morning W.G. woke up and said: 'Where are you off to, Monkey?' 'I am just going to have my cold bath.' 'Oo,' said W.G., ' 'Ow you do make me shudder!'

His dominating personality on the cricket field is well illustrated by this incident which I witnessed in a match between Lancashire and Gloucestershire. He was particularly quick to notice if any of the opponents thought the umpire was generously giving him the benefit of the doubt in an lbw decision. In this match, I was fielding first slip and an appeal from Mold who had hit the old man on the leg was disallowed. I asked Mold quietly at the end of the over his opinion of the umpire's decision, to receive an irritable reply: 'It would have sent the middle peg flying.' W.G. happened to overhear this remark and he called out: 'What's that you say, what's that you say, why you have been *throwing* at me this last half hour?' But afterwards in his calmer moments, he apologised to Mold for what he had said. Only once did W.G. put the boxing gloves on with me. On a soft wicket after hooking the slow bowler, Charles Townsend, to the out field stationed at mid wicket, I slipped and knocked my leg stump almost flat with my left foot in starting to run at the completion of my stroke. W.G. immediately shouted: ' 'E's out, 'e's out, toss 'er up, toss 'er up, 'e's out, 'e's out!' So as I was in the middle of my run I joined in the chorus, calling out to the umpire: 'I'm not out, I'm not out'—nice behaviour on the part of two international bats! When I got to the other end W.G., instead of appealing to the umpire, walked towards me with lowered head like an infuriated bull and said to me: 'Aren't you going out, Archie?' 'Not until the umpire gives me out,' I replied slowly and emphatically. Then he turned to the umpire and said: 'Well, 'ow was it?' 'Not out,' said the umpire. Then the band began to play with a vengeance, and, as I made seventy more runs after this happening, W.G. had a word for every run made, which I received in silence.

I am not going to attempt to give *all* his records (it is enough to know he established all records as a batsman and many as a bowler) but I should like to mention one or two of his best performances in some of the games in which I appeared as a member of his side or against him. If anybody has any doubt in his mind as to the best years of his life, surely the performances of W.G. from 1870 to 1876 are most convincing. In every one of these years he made a century in the Gentlemen v. Players match—on three occasions he made two separate centuries in this annual match, and on two occasions he made over two hundred in one innings. I emphasise this period because he was only twenty-two in 1870. It must not be overlooked that in spite of all this century-making W.G. got through a tremendous amount of bowling, never failing to obtain from 1874 to 1878 his hundred wickets for the season, with his wily, slow deliveries. Innumerable catches were made at deep square leg by his brother, Fred, whom the old man was always feeding with his leg breaks.

Of all my cricket mementos I prize most of all the medal given to me and to all who played in the Gentlemen v. Players match at Lord's on W.G.'s fiftieth birthday in 1898. The difficulty of the wicket was shown by this incident. I don't think in the whole of my career I would be hit on the hand by a bowler more than three times in a season. Yet in this match in the ten minutes batting I had before the luncheon interval, I was hit on the fingers three times by Lockwood, the Surrey and England fast bowler, with balls that appeared to rise straight up from the pitch and yet were well enough up to force forward play. In this match, one of the greatest in which I ever played, F. S. Jackson, Prince Ranjit and one or two more of the regulars were playing on this difficult wicket. We were in our best form and put up the score of some two hundred and fifty runs—an excellent score in the circumstances. But it was W.G. who got the highest score. That feat has always remained in my memory. It was probably the best performance of any batsman I ever saw—taking into consideration the state of the wicket and the age of the man, to say nothing of the fact that he was playing against a very fine side, including the best professional English bowlers who opened our attack in Test cricket.

At dinner that night when we had drunk to the dear old man's health, his reply as always was brief: 'Thank you, boys. If the professionals had had to bat to-day on that wicket, well, I don't think they would have done better than we did.' Then he sat down to get up again and add: 'I'm a doer, not a talker', to a chorus of 'Hear! Hear!' and 'Well spoken, old man'. This performance of the old warrior has caused me for all time to put him on a pedestal by himself. When I am asked who was the best in any department of the game, I start my reply with the words: 'Always excepting W.G. . . . ' A world famous international in his prime told me he doubted whether W.G. was quite the player he was ever made out to be. I replied, 'Wait till you are fifty when you won't look so pretty at the wicket, and then get top score in the biggest match of the year on a bowler's wicket!'

We who never saw W.G. in his prime can only guess how great he must have been in his younger days. Where he excelled in his old age, for a cricketer, was in his knowledge of the limitations imposed upon him, only by increasing years. He never attempted to do with the ball what his age prohibited, rightly preferring to *wait* for his now fewer opportunities for scoring in front of the wicket than to *make* them as he used to do in his earlier days.

He retained in a marvellous manner, almost to the last, those occasional taps through the slips off the shorter pitched ball outside the off stump, always most cleverly placed to beat the fieldsman, as well as dealing in the most telling manner with any ball on his legs which was probably the strongest feature of his batting in his palmy days.

He was rarely, if ever, at fault in throwing a 'cross' bat at the ball of driving length, or the off side. He would send it humming to the on side boundary over short mid-on's head rather than play the more orthodox stroke through the covers.

In the December of his cricketing life, when he used to captain London County, it was not too easy to get as many of the counties to play against him as he wished, owing to their already well-filled programme. On one occasion, however, Lancashire, during my captaincy, came to the rescue, gladly giving up their three days' holiday in the middle of the season to give him a game. So along came W.G. and his merry men, among them W. L. Murdoch, the famous Australian captain and batsman and a former opponent of W.G.'s. It was out of the question not to put our full strength against any side at the head of which was the old man himself, to say nothing of the presence of Billy Murdoch, who in Australia was held in the same reverence as our own champion in this country. I have the most vivid recollections of this game.

The old man won the toss from me on a perfect wicket and out stepped these two stalwarts to provide a batting treat which, at that period of their lives, was beyond all expectations. They both topped the century. It was remarkable that the effectiveness of their cutting allowed no weakening of the slip positions, thereby making their driving more telling when the bowler required that extra field on the off who could not be spared. Here was a spectacle provided by two past masters of batting whose repertoire of strokes was little less than it had been in their heyday. The conditions were perfectly suited to these two old men—sunshine in a cloudless sky, warmth in the air, and a perfect pitch beneath them. What more could they want? I am sure that no two cricketers ever enjoyed themselves more, or could have been more completely satisfied with their exhibition of batting—ever to remain a delight to those who had the fortune to witness it.

As I am speaking now, I can see W.G. and Billy Murdoch standing at the top of the steps of the pavilion as they were leaving the ground at four o'clock on the last day just as we were dismissing the end batsmen, waving and calling to me: 'Goodbye Archie', and I again call back: 'Goodbye, Billy. Goodbye, W.G.!'

Index